PHILOSOPHY OF
EXPRESSIVE ARTS THERAPY

PHILOSOPHY OF EXPRESSIVE ARTS THERAPY

Poiesis and the Therapeutic Imagination

STEPHEN K. LEVINE

FOREWORD BY CATHERINE HYLAND MOON

Jessica Kingsley *Publishers*
London and Philadelphia

Several of the essays and poems in this book have been published previously in a different form, please see the Acknowledgements for more details.

"Hope for *Poiesis*: An Interview" has been reproduced with kind permission from Paolo Knill.

First published in 2019
by Jessica Kingsley Publishers
73 Collier Street
London N1 9BE, UK
and
400 Market Street, Suite 400
Philadelphia, PA 19106, USA

www.jkp.com

Library of Congress Cataloging in Publication Data
A CIP catalog record for this book is available from the Library of Congress

British Library Cataloguing in Publication Data
A CIP catalogue record for this book is available from the British Library

ISBN 978 1 78775 005 0
eISBN 978 1 78775 006 7

Printed and bound in Great Britain

MIX
Paper from
responsible sources
FSC
www.fsc.org   FSC® C013604

To Ellen, true partner in life and art.

CONTENTS

COVER IMAGE—ARTIST'S STATEMENT

Ellen G. Levine

WHERE ARE WE GOING?

2017

This mixed-media work features a photograph which I have manipulated in various ways: cutting it up and photo-copying it many times. There are many people on a boat staring ahead while the ship ploughs through rough seas. This photograph and its enhancement lets me dream about who these people are and makes me wonder about where they are going. What do they see in the distance?

These are migrating people, in transition from one place to another. Each person has a story. They are crossing a large sea hoping to arrive somewhere safe. In the sea are possibilities—a window appears, a golden road to somewhere, colorful lights.

I have altered the photograph and used the cut-up pieces to emphasize the enormity of our situation, the large numbers of people involved in migration in the world at this time. I have also tried to introduce a quality of mystery and hopeful possibility that might exist in a journey from home to an unknown destination.

FOREWORD

Catherine Hyland Moon

Many years ago, when I graduated from college with a Bachelor of Fine Arts degree, I found myself with stacks upon stacks of my drawings, paintings, and prints. They were evidence of my accomplishments, and yet they weighed me down. While grateful for the skills I had gained, I also felt constrained by them. I was knowledgeable about the formal elements of art, able to effectively mix and apply oil paints, skilled in figure drawing, and adept at engaging in art school dialogues. But I experienced myself as unable to tap into the playful, imaginative, improvisational abilities to which I had access when I had first entered art school four years prior. The art school emphasis on skills had zapped my passion for art and disconnected me from using it as a process of meaning-making. My response to this dilemma was to do a ritual cleansing. I gave away many pieces of art to my family members and friends. Then I commenced to burn huge piles of work. It was a liberating process, yet it wasn't the total "cure" I had anticipated. It took me years to gradually reconnect with my spontaneity and artistic drive, and to bring that spontaneous energy into relational balance with the craft of art-making.

I thought of this experience while reading Stephen K. Levine's profound collection of essays and poems, which together comprise this text, *Philosophy of Expressive Arts Therapy: Poiesis and the Therapeutic Imagination*. In it, Levine proposes that the change process requires relinquishment of control over the present in order to be open to the emergent. The skills I had learned in art school enabled me to dominate tools and materials, to force them to submit to my vision of what I wanted to materialize. However, the results of my efforts, though technically successful, left me feeling hollow and dissatisfied. What I was lacking was what Levine refers to as *poiesis*, the capacity to engage creatively with what we are given in life and to shape it anew, remaking ourselves and our world in the process. My artwork-burning ritual was a way to reclaim my aesthetic right to be taken by surprise, stopped short, led by chance and circumstance into unexpected territories, and opened up to new possibilities.

Poiesis is the beating heart of this book. It is the concept around which everything else radiates, whether Levine is discussing philosophy, psychology, performance, therapy, or the state of humanity and the planet. *Poiesis* is Levine's life work, reflected through his *oeuvre* as a teacher and an author. True to the nature of this "beating heart," the essays contained herein show how Levine's ideas about the philosophy and applications of *poiesis* have continually evolved throughout his life. He demonstrates the ways in which he has been continually open to discovery. The result is that there is both a consistent theme throughout the book and a sense of freshness as new iterations of that theme are plumbed. Levine's understanding of *poiesis* is a work in progress, one marked and shaped into ever deepening iterations by the events he has experienced and the ideas he has encountered.

This book challenges arts therapists whose education has been discipline-specific to recognize the inherent connections between dance/movement, poetry, performing arts, music, and visual art. Levine's model of expressive arts therapy is centered on skillfully responding in the present moment to what is emerging, and responding to it through acts of shaping and meaning-making. For any arts therapist, it is important to recognize and respect the limits of one's scope of practice. At the same time, despite disciplinary education and training focused on a single art form, all arts therapists move, create sounds, use words to convey meaning, form identity and relationships, and respond intuitively to the world we encounter. What Levine offers is an approach through which an aesthetic way of sensing and being forms the core identity of the therapist. It is an approach that recognizes, for example, that how one's body moves (or is static) within space and how it is in relationship to other moving bodies is an essential aspect of being alive, not simply the territory of dance/movement therapists.

Engaging with this core life experience is expressed through forms as varied as conversational hand gestures and joyous explosions of movement across a dance floor. Why, the reader must ask, would any arts therapists forbid themselves from incorporating into therapy sessions even modest expressions of such a core aspect of being alive?

Levine's approach to therapeutic practice is a flexible one, responding to what is emerging in the session for the client and being ready to follow it—whether what is emerging is movement, sound, visuals, poetry, enactments, or multiple art forms. In resisting this improvisational approach, discipline-specific arts therapy practitioners are out of step with current arts practices, which are characterized by working in transdisciplinary fashion and with a generous vision of what is encompassed by the term "art." The questions faced by contemporary artists are the same for arts therapists: How much expertise in a particular art material, form, or practice is required before incorporating it with integrity into one's practice? Does a superficial engagement with an art form or practice result in a superficial practice of art or art therapy? Does restricting one's artistic vocabulary to only those materials, processes, and practices around which one can claim expertise diminish or enhance one's capability and effectiveness as an artist or art therapist? These are the kinds of compelling questions Levine's text inspires.

Another provocative topic found in Levine's essays is the proposal that art is not self-expression. He asserts that the work is what expresses, not the person; the work does not merely represent what is inside a person, but also brings something new. It has a physical, sensory presence and that presence impacts the person experiencing it. Levine's perspective challenges two commonly held notions in the arts therapies: that art is the manifestation of conscious or unconscious internal content, and that the process of creation is more important than the product. It also points to an under-developed area of research in art therapy: reception studies. Scholarship in reception studies is concerned with how people react, respond to, and interpret works of art and other cultural productions. It shifts the focus from the artist who produced the work to the participants or spectators who receive it, view it through various individual and cultural lenses, are variously affected by it, and co-create its meaning and import.

Along with theorizing the impact of artistic productions on those who witness them, Levine also considers the therapeutic environment within which those works are received. He challenges the notion that safety ought to be a dominant concern in the therapeutic space. Instead, he suggests that safety is useful only insofar as it makes possible risk-taking on the part of the client, and risk-taking is essential to effecting change. In this era of heightened awareness of individual and collective trauma and the widespread adoption of the language, if not the actual practice, of "trauma informed" care, establishing psychologically safe spaces is a common tenet of the practice of therapy. In challenging the meaning and purpose of safety for the therapy participant, Levine calls for a more complex and nuanced understanding of a taken-for-granted assumption about therapy practice.

Beyond the private encounter between therapist and therapy participant, Levine also proposes an agenda for the expressive arts therapies that includes a broad social mission, one in which the "social imaginary" is engaged for the purpose of transforming society. He believes that *poiesis*, the capacity to engage creatively with what we are given in life and to shape it anew, can be undertaken collectively, not just individually. For example, he envisions ecological change arising out of a shift in perspective by which we encounter the environment not as a natural resource but as a focus of our aesthetic responsibility. Such a shift in perspective could lead arts therapists to see fresh possibilities for our disciplines, taking us beyond the privacy of traditional therapy and out into the world where individual distress can be understood within the social systems that are often its root cause. We might, as he suggests, develop roles for creative therapists in education, coaching, consulting, conflict-transformation, and peace-building. We might see ourselves as public health workers or restorative justice practitioners. Levine challenges arts therapists to step outside our studios and consulting rooms to consider our aesthetic responsibility as citizens of our communities and our planet.

There is much to appreciate and admire about this book. Levine is able to present complex concepts from the fields of philosophy and psychology in a clear, cogent, and accessible manner. He has the rare ability to demystify discipline-specific areas of knowledge without dumbing them down. There is no pretense here, no attempt to impress the reader with academic acumen. The ideas presented have both depth and digest-ability because Levine has lived with them, contemplated them over time, experimented and played with them, and applied them to real life.

A perfect example of this application to real life can be found in how Levine approached the writing of this text. Not satisfied with merely writing about *poiesis*, he brought the concept to life by threading his own poetry throughout the book. The poems are employed not as introductions to chapters or simplistic illustrations of points he has made. Instead, the poems stand on their own, mostly without narrative explanation or contextual framing in relation to the surrounding text. Rather, they provide direct evidence of Levine's immersion in the processes he writes about. He shows us his engagement in *poiesis* through poetry.

For example, in his chapter on beauty, Levine brings his thoughts to a close by reflecting on how following the lead of one's art-making can steer one toward something newly emergent, a sort of "living beauty." Yet, the poem that follows declares, "The beauty of flowers / Is a beauty of endings / If it lasted, / Who could stand it? / Let it die / Oh, let it die." Here he playfully engages with paradoxes related to beauty: emergent versus death, newness versus ending, engagement versus detachment. In effect, his poem offers an undoing of what has preceded it; he relinquishes the neatly concluded chapter and through his poem welcomes the contradictory emergent.

Altogether, this book is a wonder! It contains the scholarly reflections of a gifted and seasoned philosopher, educator, therapist, and artist. Through this collection of essays, Stephen K. Levine pays homage to expressive arts therapy, the profession to which he has dedicated his life's work. He invites us, the readers, to engage with him in exploring the field's theoretical, practical, aesthetic, political, academic, therapeutic, and creative possibilities. What a rare treat! I highly recommend that you take him up on his invitation.

Catherine Hyland Moon
Professor, Art Therapy Department, School of the Art Institute of Chicago

ACKNOWLEDGEMENTS

I would like to thank all my students, teachers and colleagues, especially those at Lesley University in Cambridge, Massachusetts, USA; The European Graduate School in Saas Fee, Switzerland; and The Create Institute (formerly ISIS—Canada) in Toronto, Canada, as well as in other parts of the world. This book would not have been possible without them. A special thanks to Shaun McNiff and Paolo Knill, who were present at the creation of expressive arts therapy and who have stayed true to its mission since then, as well as to Elizabeth McKim, Poet Laureate of The European Graduate School, who embodies the spirit of *poiesis* in her person and in her work.

Ellen and Gabriel Levine helped with parts of the book. Donna Otter gave feedback on the first draft, and Damian Tarnopolsky helped me shape it into a whole.

Several of the essays and poems in this book appeared previously in different form. My thanks to the publishers for giving permission to reprint them here. "My Way to *Poiesis*: The Autobiography of a Concept," in *In Praise of Poiesis: The Arts and Human Existence*. "The Feast of Imagination," "Man or Beast: Imagining the Animal That I Am" (originally published as "Following the Animal That I Am") and "The Philosopher's Song," in *Poiesis: A Journal of the Arts and Communication*, 10, 2008, 11, 2009 and 13, 2011 respectively. "Beauty in Eastern and Western Thought" (originally published as "François Jullien, *This Strange Idea of the Beautiful*: A Review" and "The Tao of *Poiesis*: Chinese Philosophy and Expressive Arts" (originally published as "Expressive Arts Therapy and Taoist Philosophy") in *CAET: Creative Arts in Education and Therapy*, 4, 1, 2017, and 1, 1, 2015 respectively. "Expecting the Unexpected: The Way of Improvisation" (originally published as "Expecting the Unexpected: Improvisation in Art-Based Research") in *Journal of Applied Arts and Health*, 4, 1, 2013.

TO THE READER

The poet Paul Celan once wrote that "A poem…may be a letter in a bottle thrown out to sea with the…hope that it may somehow wash up somewhere, perhaps on the shoreline of the heart" (1999, pp.34–35). The reader of this book is unknown to me. Perhaps all books are like that. Not only is the reader unknown to the author, but even if his books have been read, the author may not be known to the reader—or, perhaps, even to himself.

What would help a reader to know a book? In this collection of essays and poems, I have also included my own story. The book is deeply personal and, thereby, universal, since we are all persons with stories to tell. I am, in part, a philosopher, a therapist, and a poet and performer. The poems and essays in this book come from my history and the identity I have shaped from it. What we come from is not who we are. As well as a past that weighs upon us, we are a future that is as yet undetermined. My understanding of *poiesis*, of our capacity for making and shaping in life and in art, is that it cannot be reduced to the past, although we must come to terms with who we have been in order to step freely into the future.

Psychotherapy has, in the main, focused on the past, and has been right to do so since unresolved suffering can hold us back from going forward. However, when past suffering is the only focus of therapeutic work, we lose sight of the possibilities that lie in every situation, no matter how dire. By putting *poiesis* at the center of my thinking about expressive arts, I have tried to cure psychotherapy of its own fixation on past experience. The personal material in this book will, I hope, give the reader some sense of how this particular author has endeavored to take what he has been given and shaped it.

In "My Way to *Poiesis*: The Autobiography of a Concept," I try to show that an idea does not come out of the blue, but arises from a life, even as it transcends it. In the section, "*Poiesis*, Therapy, and the

Arts," I go on to consider the relationship of *poiesis* to therapeutic experience. In the first essay in that section, "Expressive Arts Therapy: The Primacy of *Poiesis*," I present the basic concepts of expressive arts therapy work with individuals. In "Expressive Arts Therapy: *Poiesis* in Relationship," I look at the way in which the therapeutic relationship is central to understanding the effectiveness of a therapy grounded in the arts.

In attempting to understand the work of *poiesis*, no matter what its field of application, we must keep in mind that it includes a phase of not-knowing, one in which it is not clear how disparate elements can come together. Winnicott calls this "unintegration" and also sees it as formative in the development of the self. In "Towards the Work: Winnicott, Unintegration, and Beyond," I take this idea further and indicate that the chaotic phase of creation often leads to a form that brings things together. After all, the creative process does not rest with the experience of the creator but goes on to the making of a work.

In expressive arts, as an alternative to psychological reductionism, we take a phenomenological or descriptive approach to experience. The section "*Poiesis*: From Phenomenology to Imagination" contains several essays which reflect on the ways in which we need to go beyond a purely descriptive method of our experience to one that includes the imagination, which is, after all, at the basis of art-making. "The Feast of Imagination" shows the profusion of images that arise in our daily life. In "Image Work: Imaginal Psychology and the Expressive Arts" there is a presentation and critique of the imaginal psychology of James Hillman, whose writing is a paean to the power of the imagination. "Man or Beast: Imagining the Animal that I Am" begins with Jacques Derrida's deconstruction of the traditional binary distinction between human and animal and then considers an imaginative way of thinking about that difference (or *différance*, as Derrida might put it) by the novelist J.M. Coetzee. Finally, "The Philosopher's Song" questions the traditional opposition between discursive thought and imaginative art by asking philosophy itself to sing.

"The Way of *Poiesis*: A Chinese Perspective" includes two essays on art and therapy from the point of view of classical Chinese thought, providing an alternative to traditional Western ideas.

"Beauty in Eastern and Western Thought" shows another way of thinking about beauty, the central concept of Western aesthetics, and "The Tao of *Poiesis*: Chinese Philosophy and Expressive Arts" gives us a different approach to understanding the relationship of art and life, one based on *wu-wei* or non-doing.

The next section, "*Poiesis*, Improvisation, Identity," explores several of the themes contained in the previous writings. If we give up the comfort of an already established procedure, what is left? "Expecting the Unexpected: The Way of Improvisation," based primarily on my experience in artistic performance, considers improvisation as a way of going beyond method that is similar to *wu-wei*. In not-knowing and not-controlling our behavior according to a plan, surprising results may occur. At the same time, these results may also create new problems to respond to. "Keep Your Shirt On!: Art, Therapy, and the Space In-Between" reflects on the complex relationship between art and therapy when the roles and responsibilities differ in the two realms, especially when the issue of safety arises out of improvised and surprising behavior. In "Who am I? What am I?: The *Poiesis* of Identity" I raise the question of the place of improvisation in the formation of selfhood. Does the identity of the person itself arise from improvisatory behavior, and is this a form of *poiesis*? What then becomes of what is commonly known as "identity politics?"

I am sure that no one will ever have the last word on these tangled matters. However, there must always be last words in a book, as in a life—and these may also concern final or ultimate things. "Last Words: When All is Said and Done" begins with a reflection on the role of the arts in coming to terms with trauma and loss, especially in mourning. Can the arts do justice to extreme suffering? "The Art of Trauma: *Poiesis* and Human Existence" considers how the power of *poiesis* in confronting loss depends on the extent to which it recognizes finitude as essential to art, as well as to life. Only if *poiesis* includes a sense of its own temporal finitude can it be equal to the experience of loss.

What then can we hope for at the end? In "Hope for *Poiesis*: An Interview," a conversation between Paolo Knill and myself held at the European Graduate School in the summer of 2018, the power of *poiesis* emerges in surprising ways. What more can we hope for than to experience our capacity to be in the world with others in a creative way? This is, perhaps, a fragile hope, but perhaps for that very reason one worth holding on to.

A book about *poiesis* should, I believe, have itself a poietic quality. For that reason, I have included several of my poems after the more discursive essay writing. I hope that, even if my thinking does not persuade, the poetry will at least show that I have tried to confront the joys and sorrows of human life with the power of *poiesis*.

This book indeed stems from a faith in *poiesis*, the capacity to respond to what is given and to shape it creatively, using a sense of beauty as our guide. Does this collection of heterogeneous writings form a cohesive whole? Must wholeness be cohesive, if fragmentation is part of its coming into being? *Poiesis* necessarily includes a chaotic or unintegrated phase in which the imagination is given free play. I hope that some of that unintegrated quality remains in this book. May the reader be inspired by this work to create new forms of their own adequate to the challenges they face in therapy, art and life.

INVOCATION

Take your tall body up
and let it stand.
You were not born
for bending. Neck bowed.
Chest caved in. Cowering before
the world. Nay,
stand tall to tell
the tale. See those
to whom you speak
and sing
at last.

MY WAY TO *POIESIS*: THE AUTOBIOGRAPHY OF A CONCEPT

Life, to paraphrase Kierkegaard, can only be understood backwards; but it must be lived forward (1999, p.3). In the living of it, we do not know where we are going. Afterwards, perhaps, we can see a pattern emerging from what we have left behind, the traces of the path we have taken. The temptation, then, is to attribute this understanding to the past and give the meaning that we find in retrospect the status of a cause, the determinant of our acts.

When I look back on my life and my thinking, I see an erratic path, a wandering without a destination, one that nevertheless arrives. Is this resting-point a destiny or merely a stop along the way? Perhaps the answer to that question will only reveal itself to a later gaze. Nevertheless I see that I am at a place I call *poiesis*, a Greek word that I have appropriated for my own purposes. *Poiesis* surely retains its original signification of "making" in general and of the special kind of making we call "art" and the Greeks called "poetry" (a significant difference in itself) in particular, but the word has for me a different connotation and value than it had in those writings of Plato and Aristotle in which it first appeared as an object of philosophical reflection. It is my hope that this different way of thinking will be helpful to those who come after me, if only as something they too can surpass.

Poiesis, in my sense of the term, is the crystallization of a series of life experiences which range from the theoretical to the practical to the aesthetic. I will try in these pages to trace the path that led me to this idea, with the awareness that even this act of reflective self-awareness is a poietic one, a making sense out of the material of what has gone before. It is therefore itself another step in a journey of *poiesis,* and one, I hope, that may lead to new destinations and other paths to explore.

I was born in Brooklyn, New York, in 1938, to a middle-class Jewish family. This means, among other things, that my early childhood was lived in a society emerging from an economic depression and subsequently engaged in a Great War. I was very much aware of the war as a child and remember preparing for the imminent Japanese invasion by joining with my friends and urinating into a number of glass jars, storing them in my basement to be used as weapons (a home-grown version of what came to be called the "Molotov cocktail"). I also remember lying in my bed at night, obsessed with fantasies of traveling through time and assassinating Hitler before he could begin his campaign of extermination of the Jews.

There was no mention of the Holocaust in my family; my father kept his counsel and my mother adhered to the old Jewish motto, "Don't tell the children," itself a kind of charm to protect against danger. At the same time, my favorite radio program was called "The Shadow," the narrator of which began each episode by intoning in a deep voice, "Who knows what evil lurks in the hearts of men? The Shadow knows." I was drawn to this notion of a hidden underside to things and longed to be the one to come to know it.

My family was not artistic or bohemian. My father was a hard-working businessman who left the house each morning to travel by subway and train to Westchester, where he owned what came to be a number of small supermarkets. As the second son and youngest child, I was somewhat immune from pressure to join the family business. I recall coming down from my room at age ten or thereabouts and solemnly announcing that when I grew up, I would not go into business. I also remember not being sure exactly what the word, "business," meant. I only knew I wasn't going to do it.

I was brought to Broadway shows with my parents after the war and was impressed by the dynamism of the performers, especially Ethel Merman in *Annie Get Your Gun,* who bore an uncanny resemblance to my mother. (I later played Ethel Merman in a cabaret show at The European Graduate School.) At night I would secretly listen to the radio in my room after bedtime, entranced by the verbal meanderings of Jean Shepherd on his late-night show and listening avidly to the black station that played rhythm and blues. Somehow the R&B singer Ruth Brown spoke to me in ways that my own culture seemed unaware of.

It was not until I went to university, however, that the arts began to have meaning for my life. In 1956 America was in the grip of the Cold War and McCarthyism. I felt profoundly disaffected from the preoccupations of the other students at the university, which seemed to focus on football and fraternities. I began to write poetry as a way through my despair and ultimately became the editor of the *Pennsylvania Literary Review*, the first in a series of journals I would later edit, including *POIESIS: A Journal of the Arts and Communication*. My fellow writers at university were as alienated as I was, and we formed a small band of outsiders, even keeping a distance from the few self-identified Beats, whose black turtlenecks seemed to us to be yet another badge of conformity. I did, however, fall in love with Allen Ginsberg's *Howl!* Its anguished prophetic cry seemed to give voice to my own disaffection. Kerouac's *On the Road* stirred me as well; the mobile flow of language promised an alternative to the enforced stasis of official American life.

I also began to become politically active, taking part in Ban the Bomb demonstrations and joining the War Resisters' League, an anarcho-pacifist group. Anarchism seemed to me to be the one political movement that could account for the essential disorder of society hidden beneath its bureaucratic surface. For the same reason I became a strong critic of the Soviet Union and was outraged when onlookers would shout at us at demonstrations, "Go back to Russia!" I was attracted to non-violent civil disobedience as a form of protest and would later see the civil rights and anti-war movements as embodying the spirit of anarchic revolt. A culminating moment came after university when I moved back to New York and participated in the General Strike for Peace, a rather ambitious project spearheaded by Julian Beck and Judith Malina, founders of the Living Theater, an avant-garde theatrical troupe. When we were all arrested at a sit-in in Times Square in 1962, we felt sure that our movement would spread to the public-at-large. Perhaps in a way it did.

While at university, I harbored dreams of dropping-out and dedicating myself to becoming a poet, but I was held back by fear of losing my student deferment and consequently being drafted into the army. (I would later escape the draft by engaging in my first theatrical role; that of a schizoid young man who, as my first wife's psychiatrist—also President Nixon's —said "would demoralize a regiment.") In effect, I had dropped out, not attending classes, skipping examinations and ultimately failing a number of courses. In frustration, the dean of the university gave me an ultimatum: either I went into therapy or I would be expelled. At the time, I saw this as a form of mind-control, but in fact it inaugurated a life-long interest in the psyche and in attempts to heal its distress. I had the good fortune to be referred by the university to a psychoanalytic psychotherapist, Lester Luborsky, who was, above all else, a good listener and who gave me the sense that my story had meaning and value, even if it didn't fit into any normal pattern.

In later years I would see therapists of all stripes, ranging from Kurt Adler, Alfred Adler's son (the only therapist I ever had who seemed more radical politically than I was!) to art therapists, Gestalt and bioenergetic therapists, practitioners of psychodrama, psychosynthesis, Jungian analysis, and others. It seems to me sometimes that I have lived a life in therapy, and yet I believe, as Freud did, that there is no end to it; we can always go further in our self-understanding. Oddly enough, perhaps, I have not become disillusioned. Indeed, I celebrate all my therapists and all those who seek to heal others. This is a noble task, even if it must ultimately fail.

As I began to find a greater measure of self-acceptance through therapy, I sought an academic path that would have space for my alternative vision of the world. I was drawn to Taoism and Buddhism, which was then, in the 1950s, just emerging into cultural awareness in the West. I found in the Taoist notion of *wu-wei*, non-action, an indication of a different way of being in the world. Rather than the imposition of an idea or an ideology from above, Taoism seemed to offer a vision of action from below, from emerging from nothingness and from letting-go. I decided to major in what was then called "Oriental Studies" at the University of Pennsylvania and spent several years immersed in classical Chinese and Japanese culture, learning Chinese and trying to understand a way of life that seemed profoundly different from the one my own culture offered. Ultimately, though, I came to the conclusion that Chinese

Communism had destroyed what I valued most in Chinese culture and that I was pursuing a mere antiquarian interest rather than a living tradition.

I began to read contemporary European philosophy and was especially drawn to the writings of Heidegger and Sartre, sensing that what I understood as their conception of nothingness was akin to both the Taoist and Buddhist notion of the Void. I decided to stay in school and study Western philosophy. By chance, I was directed by a friend to the New School for Social Research in New York, where I began graduate work in philosophy in 1962. The Graduate Faculty of Political and Social Science at the New School was in fact the ideal intellectual environment for me at the time. Founded in the late 1930s as the University in Exile, a haven for refugee European scholars, the Graduate Faculty had preserved the European tradition of thought that had been, at least temporarily, destroyed by Hitler. From the moment I walked into my first class and heard Hans Jonas lecture on Kant's *Critique of Pure Reason*, I knew I had found a home, though in truth I understood barely a word.

It was my good fortune to have been at the Graduate Faculty of the New School before it became well-known. Classes were quite small and there was direct personal contact between students and professors. The philosophy department was staffed by former students of Husserl and Heidegger, and there was a sense of the direct transmission of the phenomenological tradition, as well as a thorough grounding in the history of Western philosophy. It's good to recall, now that "theory" in its European form has become dominant (though perhaps already passé) in the academy, how "outside" this tradition seemed to be to American thought, dominated at the time by logical positivism and ordinary language philosophy in philosophy departments, and by a naïve pragmatism in popular culture. Once again, I found myself drawn to alternative pathways, an exile in my own land.

I spent several years in the philosophy department at the New School, absorbing the tradition to the best of my ability and trying to find my own direction. Through the teaching of Werner Marx (later to become Heidegger's successor at the University of Freiburg), I became fascinated by Heidegger's later thinking, especially his essay on the origin of the work of art, and decided to do my dissertation on an interpretation of that important work. In particular I saw a connection between Heidegger's concept of authentic existence in *Being and Time* and his thinking about the coming into being of the work of art in his later writings. At last, it seemed to me, I had found a ground for my intuition that poetic existence was indeed more authentic than what passed for normal behavior in the dominant culture at that time. Heidegger's former political support of Nazism did not deter me then; it was only later, when the full extent of his involvement became known, that an awareness of the problematical relationship between his life and thought came into general awareness.

My instructors, however, had directly experienced Heidegger's betrayal of his own teacher, Edmund Husserl, the founder of phenomenology. Rather than seeing Heidegger as one who continued and modified the phenomenological tradition in an essential way, they viewed him as an heretic whose work was fundamentally flawed. As a result, Aron Gurwitsch refused to supervise my thesis on Heidegger, and Hans Jonas agreed to do so only if I framed my interpretation within a critical perspective. I am not certain that I could do this well even at the present time, but certainly I was not equipped to do so then. The result was a bit of a mish-mash, some insightful interpretations framed by an inadequate critique. Perhaps we are all still trying to find the path of "thinking after Heidegger," as the title of David Wood's book indicates (2002), that appropriates what we need but goes on to find new directions.

My first full-time academic position was in 1967 at Duquesne University in Pittsburgh, a center of phenomenological study. While at Duquesne, however, my involvement in the anti-war movement increased. I joined the Students for a Democratic Society and helped form a chapter at the university, and I ultimately became involved in a protest against the university administration, partly based upon its decision to issue the toxic chemical Mace to campus guards to control what some feared would be an invasion from the adjacent black community. In the end, I resigned in protest during my second year of teaching at Duquesne and returned to New York. Unable to secure employment as a professor (Gurwitsch swore he would make sure I'd never get an academic job again), I decided to pursue another of my disparate interests and undertake a post-doctoral degree in anthropology at the New School, studying primarily with Stanley Diamond.

I had earlier been tangentially involved in the nascent Native American movement through my first wife's connections and, like many at the time, saw the tradition of indigenous culture as a possible alternative to the dominance of liberal capitalism. Diamond was a poet/anthropologist who had focused his work on the concept of the "primitive" as a touchstone for a critique of contemporary civilization. While studying with him, I founded the journal *Critical Anthropology*, which shared this vision of using indigenous traditions to criticize the contemporary world. I also became influenced by the emerging communal movement in North America and saw it as embodying Heideggerean notions of community.

When the bombing of Cambodia by the United States government began, Diamond gathered those he saw as student leaders and urged us to initiate a protest at the school. This ultimately led to the takeover and occupation of the New School by radical graduate students, an event in the spirit of the May revolt of 1968 in Paris and one which, I believe, was equally transformative for its participants. The occupation, which was as much a cultural as a political revolt, lasted for several weeks, until a group of the faculty, led by my old philosophy professors, called the police and had those of us who refused to leave arrested. As I walked out of the building, my last words to Professor Gurwitsch were, "The transcendental reduction sucks!" by which I meant to indicate that philosophy had to find its place in the world and not be situated in a transcendent realm of knowledge. In retrospect, my break with my own teachers now appears to me as a tragic but necessary event, a collision of two worlds. Today I would pay them respect for their integrity and devotion to philosophic thought, while at the same time I continue to honor the impulse of protest against violence and injustice that led me to go a different way.

The strike at the New School seems to me now a turning-point in my life. In a peaceful time (if there ever were peaceful times), I would have continued in the tradition of my teachers and probably taken their place in this lineage. I often think it was my destiny to be a Professor of Philosophy at the Graduate Faculty of the

New School, but history cares nothing for destiny and deposits us where it will. In the end, after a brief period teaching philosophy at Rutgers University in Newark (having found a position there despite Gurwitsch's vow), and after a failed attempt at founding a political commune in Peekskill, New York, my then and current partner Ellen Levine and I moved to Canada and began teaching at York University in Toronto.

Although the move to York was primarily for professional reasons (York offered the promise of interdisciplinary teaching and of participating in the formation of the new Graduate Programme in Social and Political Thought), I also see it as an expression of the disappointment and disaffection both Ellen and I felt at the time in America. We were *émigrés malgré nous*, and we lived the dislocated life that all emigrants engage in. What was envisioned as a brief hiatus, a break from the collective madness of American society, became a four-decade long sojourn, with the establishment of a more or less permanent home, careers and family. At the same time, I have never ceased longing for my home, that yet-to-be identified place where I belong and which perhaps does not exist.

In many ways, Toronto has been good to us. My position at York was so interdisciplinary that I could begin to incorporate all my interests—philosophical, aesthetic and therapeutic—into it. Ellen had started to study at the Toronto Art Therapy Institute, and I soon joined her, first as a client and then as a teacher of psychoanalytic theory. Dr. Martin Fisher, the Director of the Institute, had introduced art therapy into Ontario. He was a Jewish immigrant from Austria who looked and sounded exactly as we imagined Freud did. Dr. Fisher was a warm and affectionate presence who ruled his Institute as a beneficent authority figure from his office on the third floor, interpreting the paintings that his students and clients, under the guidance of female graduates, had made in the basement of the building. This hierarchical and patriarchal architecture reflected not only the position of Dr. Fisher in relation to his students and clients but also the relation of psychoanalytic theory to art-making. The art-work was seen as having an underlying meaning that only an analytical interpretation could reveal. It helped that Dr. Fisher was a compassionate and kindly authority, but in the end I felt once again that I needed to find my own path. My bottom-up ways of thinking and acting did not fit with the top-down structure of the Institute, which seemed to me to be antithetical to the spirit of art-making itself.

After a year in a humanistic psychotherapy training program in Cambridge, Massachusetts, in 1976–77, I began to study at the Toronto Institute of Human Relations (TIHR), a pastoral counseling training center which operated within a broadly eclectic therapeutic framework. In spite of its Christian atmosphere, I felt very much at home at TIHR. Its emphasis on experiential education fit with my own predilections, and its experimental and open-ended approach to therapeutic theory and practice gave me an appreciation for the range of possibilities of human development and change. I stayed at TIHR for six years, as an Intern, Resident and Supervising Consultant and ultimately returned in the mid-80s for two years as a Training Director.

While teaching philosophy and social science at York and training in psychotherapy at TIHR, I was also engaged in studying theater at various venues in Toronto. I had discovered a love of performance in the early 1970s and participated in a series of workshops in experimental and avant-garde theater that seemed to me to embody the same spirit that I had found in my therapy training. My performance work ultimately led me into involvement with what was called "physical theater," culminating in an intensive clown workshop with Philippe Gaulier in Toronto and then training and collaborating with Kaf Warman in clown and *commedia dell'arte* productions in Martha's Vineyard (where Ellen and I had vacationed and subsequently built a home in 1984). I continued to work with both Philippe and Kaf over the years. They had both been trained and influenced by Jacques Lecoq, the legendary teacher of physical theater in Paris. Lecoq's work revived traditions of popular theater that had been neglected by the dominant culture and restored the primacy of the body and movement to a performance tradition dominated by the language of the text. Ellen later trained with Richard Pochinko, a Lecoq graduate who was also influenced by his work with Grotowski and by native shamanic traditions. Together we gradually discovered our own clown couple, Max and Sadie, an old Jewish twosome who strangely enough seemed to embody some of our own most ridiculous aspects.

By the mid-80s, then, I was living in three worlds: the academic, the therapeutic and the artistic. To me, there was a common thread that bound them all. My teaching at the university focused on the aesthetic and therapeutic dimensions, my therapeutic practice was becoming more action- and art-oriented, and my theater work shared a spirit of experimentation and exploration with both my thinking and my therapeutic practice; yet I lacked a place, either physical or cultural, where I could put them all together. It was at this point that I made the fortunate decision to spend a year at the Institute for the Arts and Human Development at Lesley College (now Lesley University) in Cambridge, studying what was then called "Expressive Therapy" as a post-doctoral fellow. In truth, I knew nothing about the program and had never met anyone in it; but somehow I was drawn to what it seemed to offer. And indeed Lesley became the place where all my interests converged and where I could find a new path to follow that would be worth exploring for years to come.

I had intended to study psychodrama at Lesley, but when I told the Dean of the Arts Institute, Shaun McNiff, of my intention, he insisted I meet Paolo Knill, a colleague of his who might have something of interest to offer me. Like my experience at the New School, as soon as I met Paolo, I knew I was in the right place. Not only was he an accomplished artist and therapist, but his broad European cultural background and interests gave him a perspective within which he could situate the varied aspects of my own work. We immediately began talking about Heidegger and initiated a friendship and working relationship that has persisted to this day. From Paolo and Shaun, I learned the theory and practice of intermodal expressive therapy, something which, like the character in Molière who was astounded to discover that all his life he had been speaking prose, I discovered I had been doing myself all these years. The creative community that these innovators established formed a rare and valuable cultural moment, reminiscent of Black Mountain College in its earlier days and a premonition of the European Graduate School today. My year at Lesley was truly life-changing, and I remain grateful for the new direction it gave me. Through my work with Elizabeth McKim, I also reaffirmed my love of poetry and was able to connect it with the oral tradition of performance in which it had originated. Elizabeth continues to inspire me to this day.

Upon my return to Toronto, I began to develop a proposal for a new MA program in interdisciplinary arts therapy, at the invitation of the Dean of Fine Arts at York. I subsequently spent three years developing the proposal, gathering support and shepherding it through eight committees, only in the end to have it be rejected for what seemed to me to be bureaucratic and territorial grounds. Perhaps, however, this was, like my departure from the New School, another *felix culpa*, a fortunate fall. While traveling with Paolo to a conference in Europe, I stopped at a weekend seminar of the ISIS-Switzerland expressive therapy training program he had established in Zurich. It suddenly struck me that I could start a similar program in Toronto. With the collaboration of Ellen and Fran Harwood, a psychotherapist colleague in Toronto, I helped found ISIS-Canada, now called The Create Institute, in 1991. In many ways, the program at CREATE gave me and many others much more than the university could have offered. Freed from bureaucratic constraints and turf-battles, the institute was able to carry out its training in an innovative and creative spirit appropriate to the field of expressive arts therapy itself. Though times have changed and CREATE is now established on the Canadian scene, I believe some of that original spirit still persists today, even as psychotherapy becomes more and more regulated.

In 1996, Paolo Knill established the European Graduate School (EGS) in Switzerland and invited both Ellen and me to join him as teachers and, in fact, co-creators. Together, with Margo Fuchs and Majken Jacoby from Denmark, we taught the first EGS summer school in a non-stop intensive burst of creative energy. Our program was soon joined by one in Media and Communication, founded by Wolfgang Schirmacher, with whom I shared a common philosophical background. Over the years EGS has become an established institution, but I believe we have to a great extent avoided the dangers of routinization to which the establishment of something new usually leads. I like to think that the spirit of '68 lives at EGS as well. "Power to the Imagination" is a motto with, I believe, enduring relevance, as I hope this book will show.

As my teaching and practice of what we came to call "expressive arts therapy" has evolved, I have tried to develop a theoretical perspective adequate to the work. In my first book, *Poiesis: The Language of Psychology and the Speech of the Soul* (Levine 1997), I drew on Heidegger but also on the work of D.W. Winnicott and Victor Turner to formulate an initial conception of *poiesis*. Heidegger's thinking of human existence as being-in-the-world, a being without a transcendent foundation on which to rely and which therefore had to make a new world through its poietic acts, seemed to me to resonate with Winnicott's notion of transitional experience and Turner's concept of liminality. In all of these, there is the sense of dwelling in uncertainty without the possibility of absolute knowledge, quite different from the Cartesian search for an indubitable starting point and from subsequent philosophies grounded on theoretical reason. Human experience often takes place under the sign of not-knowing; it requires, as Jack Weller has put it, "planting your feet firmly in nothingness" (1993, p.103) and being willing to welcome and explore this unknown as a fertile field of play. Out of the fragments of what has been given us, we can build new worlds, not as final resting-grounds, but as offerings to a future yet to be determined.

Unlike traditional conceptions of *poiesis* as the imposition of an idea upon inert matter, I conceived of the poietic act as emergent, something which comes from the exploration of a situation, an experiment which seeks to come up with what is effective, what "works." Certainly *poiesis* culminates in form, but it does not begin there, and even the structures which emerge are but building blocks which have to be taken apart so that a new order can emerge. *Poiesis*, then is a deconstructive act, one that takes apart the tradition, that which has been handed down, but one that forms new traditions themselves ready to be transcended. In praise of *poiesis*, I would thus offer up the toast "Bottoms up!"

In this sense, life is indeed lived forward and understood, if at all, only afterwards. We are makers of worlds, but unlike the deity, we do not know what we are making. We are devoid of the certainty and security which indubitable knowledge would bring, but in its place we have the joy of discovery, the possibility of participation in the creation of something new. In this spirit I have written in praise of *poiesis* and hope that my readers will discover for themselves both the possibility of a rebirth of wonder and a love of the work.

ETHEL MERMAN WAS MY MOTHER

Belting it out,
"I can do anything better than you."
Built to be placed on the prow of a ship,
Ethel invincible,
Victorious.
Was there ever any doubt she would win?

Even with the anguish in her voice.
Even with the crying out to heaven
For release from pain,
Even with the screaming in the chambers
That no one heard.

Her voice on stage pierces me.
And I see angels ask forgiveness
For their crimes.

Sing out, my darling.
Even now I hear you
Through the generations

My own terrible angel
Of the night.

PART I

POIESIS, THERAPY, AND THE ARTS

1

EXPRESSIVE ARTS THERAPY

THE PRIMACY OF *POIESIS*

Expressive arts therapy has continued to develop since its beginnings in the 1970s. The basis for theory and clinical practice has been clarified and elaborated, and the field itself has expanded beyond the therapeutic realm. I would like to briefly outline some of these developments and explain the significance of *poiesis* in understanding the framework of the therapeutic process in the expressive arts.

On the theoretical level, the basic concept of *poiesis* has been deepened and extended in order to provide a better foundation for expressive arts practice. *Poiesis* is the ancient Greek word for making. It was used especially to refer to art-making, the production of works of art. Through further reflection on this basic concept, it became clear to me that the activity of *poiesis* not only refers to art-making but is basic to human existence. Human beings are not born pre-adapted to their environment, as other animal species are. Instead they have to find ways to respond to the world in which they find themselves, and then find ways to shape it so that it can become an appropriate place in which they can live. Shaping what is given is what I mean by *poiesis*.

This basic activity of shaping in response to what is given is, I believe, characteristic of human beings at all times of history and in all kinds of culture. Our very existence in this world is an act of shaping or *poiesis*. Of course, this does not mean that we always shape things in a good way. We may create worlds that are destructive to ourselves, to others and to the environment which surrounds us. For this reason, we often need help in finding more creative and appropriate ways to respond to what has been given to us. This is the role of what we call the "change agent," whether in therapy or in social and environmental change.

The human being is an embodied being in the world. We experience this world through the senses before we are able to understand it intellectually. The senses not only give us bodily impressions, they also make sense and indicate where to take action. "Aesthetics" as a philosophical discipline is usually thought of as restricted to the study of our experience of works of art. However, the Greek word *aisthesis* originally meant, "pertaining to the senses." Sensing can thus be considered to be an aesthetic activity, a mode of human existence that grasps the world as embodied form. When the form of the world strikes us as pleasing and meaningful, we experience it as beautiful.

Beauty, then, can be considered as a criterion for all our acts of shaping the world in which we live. We do not wish to live in an "an-aesthetic" world, one that makes no sense; rather we find happiness in our capacity to shape the world so that we can bring beauty into being. In the field of expressive arts, we call this our "aesthetic responsibility." It is the aesthetic responsibility of the change agent to help the person or community with whom they are working to use, their capacity to shape their world, so that it brings about beauty in their lives. (The concept of aesthetic responsibility and the following presentation of the basic principles of expressive arts, and the framework of the architecture of the session, is based upon my own conception of *poiesis* and on the work of Paolo Knill.) (Knill, Levine and Levine 2005)

Poiesis in the special sense of art-making is a particularly appropriate way to achieve this goal. The arts are not only things that are made (paintings, poems, dramas, music, etc.); they are things that show themselves as being made. Ordinarily the things around us present themselves as being of use: we drive our cars, type on our computers, etc., without much thought for the things themselves, unless they break, and then we are usually interested in repairing them and getting them back to being useful.

However, the work of art does not disappear in its utility; rather it demands to be seen for its own sake. As a result, it can have a powerful effect upon us, an effect that we call an aesthetic response, the experience of having our breath taken away and feeling moved or touched. The aesthetic responsibility of the change agent is thus to help the person(s) with whom they are working to find their aesthetic response.

This powerful capacity of aesthetic response is especially strong when it is a consequence of the person's own actions. In that case, it is not only the work of art that is effective but the very experience of art-making, of having the capacity to shape the material that is given, that restores the person to their authentic existence as a human being, a being for whom *poiesis* is essential. If we can have the experience of shaping and bringing forth beauty through the arts in a therapeutic or other specialized setting, then we can take the capacities that have been awakened and bring them back into our daily experience. Art-making is continuous with living; it is the same person who engages in an expressive arts session and who lives in the world with others as a life partner, a worker, a citizen, etc. The families, workplaces and countries in which we live are shaped by human activity, our own or others; therefore they can be re-formed in ways that are more appropriate.

What is it about art-making that is so powerful? In order to be able to find new forms, we need to go beyond our everyday concerns and enter the world of imagination. This is an experience of what we call decentering from the world of everyday life in order to enter the world of imagination. As the field of expressive arts has deepened and clarified its foundations, it has become clear that decentering is an essential moment in the process of *poiesis* (Knill *et al.* 2005). An expressive arts session, then, might begin with a clarification of the basic concern or problem that the person or group has; but then it has to decenter from those concerns into the alternative world of the imagination in order to find more room to play. Only after this process of decentering into the imagination through art-making has been carried through can we return to the world of everyday life and reflect on what we have learned.

In expressive arts, we do not undertake this reflective process from a pre-established psychological framework, as do many of the other arts therapies, which base their understanding upon previously established psychological theories that understand art as a representation of an already existing psychic state.

Rather, art-making involves a process of discovery that introduces something new into the world. Psychological reductionism, seeing the present in terms of the past, cannot explain this creative emergence.

Therefore, we let the work and the acts of shaping it show themselves to us by themselves. In adopting what we can call a phenomenological attitude of paying careful attention to what has occurred, we can allow the work and the shaping process to speak for themselves and, in this way, teach us something we may not already know. We can then "harvest" the session, i.e., reflect on the ways that what has happened may have something to do with our everyday lives and give us a new direction for action in the future.

Based on the primacy of *poiesis*, Knill has formulated what he calls the "architecture" of the session" (Knill *et al.* 2005, p.94), a basic framework that can be used to understand the work we are doing in any setting. First comes the "filling-in," the clarification of the literal situation in which the client or group finds themselves. We need to know what the problem is, how the person has been able to deal with this kind of thing in the past, and what sort of outcome they would like to have from the session. Note that although we do need to understand the difficulty or concern, we do not, in accordance with our capacity for *poiesis*, focus primarily on the suffering or pathology but look for the creative resources that the person may have, those which, under the pressure of their situation, they may not have been able to utilize. In this sense, we could say that expressive arts is "resource-oriented" and "solution-focused."

At this point in a session, however, we need to step away or "decenter" from filling-in about the concerns of everyday life, the "tight spot" in which the person finds themself, in order to step into the world of the imagination through play, art-making or ritual. The therapist or change agent has the aesthetic responsibility of shaping the session for the client so that the latter can have an aesthetic response, an experience of beauty through their capacity to shape the materials with which they are working. There is no pre-given method for the interventions of the therapist; rather they must use their sensitivity to see what is effective for the particular person with whom they are working, what affects them or touches what we call, following H.G. Gadamer's concept of effective history, their "effective reality" (2004, p.267).

Once this is accomplished, it is possible to step back from the decentering and describe it from a phenomenological perspective, paying careful attention to both the process and the product and letting each of them give us the message they may contain. Since the decentering has taken place in the presence of the change agent, they may join the client in the careful descriptions that go into this aesthetic analysis.

After an adequate analysis of the decentering, we need to find a bridge back to the concerns that the client has brought into the session. Asking for a title and a message in the decentering may help. If the aesthetic analysis has been adequately accomplished, the relevance of the decentering to the person's life will often be obvious. It may also help to ask, "If what happened in the decentering has something to do with the concern which you presented earlier, what might that be?" By asking a hypothetical question, the imagination is brought into play even in the reflection on literal reality.

Thus the architecture of the session consists in the phases of filling-in, decentering, aesthetic analysis and harvesting. Note that these phases may not be sequential. Sometimes a client will come in to the session wanting to make art, and only later will they talk about their concerns. Moreover, in any particular session, some of these phases may be absent. After a filling-in and an extended decentering, for example, there may not be time for the aesthetic analysis or harvesting. These can then be the subject of a subsequent session.

In addition, when working with certain kinds of clients, the filling-in and harvesting have to be done with others. This could be the case with children or adults of diminished capacity. In these instances, the filling-in and harvesting might be done by the parents, teachers or other care-givers, either before the session or after. The aesthetic analysis, of course, can only be done with someone who has the capacity for reflection. If this capacity is absent, the therapist might carry it out on her own in order to better understand the implications of the decentering.

The "architecture of the session" is more of a map than a method; it enables the therapist or other change agent to locate where they are at any given point and what kinds of interventions are appropriate. The important thing to remember is that working in the expressive arts is based on *poiesis*: the capacity of human beings to enter into the world of imagination and to engage in a process of art-making that will result in an aesthetic response, one that brings about a meaningful change in the person's sense of self and world. *Poiesis* is our primary capacity; everything follows from this.

As the concept of *poiesis* has been deepened and clarified, my colleagues and I have also extended it to other realms. Expressive arts began as a therapeutic approach. However, understanding the philosophical foundations of expressive arts has shown us that the basic principles of this work can be extended beyond the therapeutic realm to fields as diverse as education, coaching, consulting, and social and environmental change. In all these fields, the activity of *poiesis* is primary. Whether it is a question of our schools, our organizations, or our societies and environments, in each case we are given a world that has been already made; it is our responsibility to shape it anew.

In society as a whole, social and environmental concerns have begun to replace those stemming from individual psychology as the dominant focus of attention. We realize more and more how much our experience is not just our own but depends on the world and others around us. Expressive arts practitioners have opened new perspectives for using the arts to work with the effects of traumatic situations that have been brought about through social or political events (Levine and Levine 2011). Indeed, even the natural environment, its depredation and capacity for renewal, can be seen as a field for the practice of expressive arts (Levine 2017).

As expressive arts therapy has matured, its theoretical and practical foundations have been deepened, clarified and extended. However, it remains for future generations to take this work and find new directions in which it can be developed. The human capacity for *poiesis* can never be exhausted. It is our responsibility to continue to bring beauty into the world and to shape ourselves and our social and natural environments in a way that makes sense. Only thus can we hope to find fulfillment and happiness in this life.

PATRÍA

So much beauty! We must look.
"How can I tell you what is in my heart?
Impossible to begin. Enough.
No. Begin."[1]

All that love. All that longing.
Seventy-five young bodies on the floor.
Raised platforms. Young actors telling their stories of Perú.

Tania sits in front of her family's photograph.
Images fade. Only the Quechua grandmother's face
*   remains.*
Her song fills the room.

Oh, they loved their country,
loved it in a way we have forgotten,
loved it not as idea but as flesh, as matter.
Loved it so much they became furious,
striking out at the ones who betrayed the dream:
Candidates. Faces. Voices. Simulacra.

So much beauty! So much love!
How can I tell you what is in my heart?
No. Begin. We must look.
Begin.

---

1   Maira Kalman (2007), *The Principles of Uncertainty*, p.3. New York: The Penguin
Press.

2

EXPRESSIVE ARTS THERAPY

POIESIS IN RELATIONSHIP

Expressive arts therapy needs to understand *poiesis* not only in terms of the art that may emerge, but also in terms of the relationship between the therapist and the client in which the act of creation takes place. We have written about the role of the therapist in terms of the concept of aesthetic responsibility, but the specifically relational character of the therapeutic relationship in expressive arts therapy needs to be considered further, especially in the light of the fact that much of contemporary psychotherapy considers itself relational. I will briefly outline the development of the relational aspect of expressive arts therapy, beginning with Freud and culminating in D.W. Winnicott's concept of transitional experience that occurs in play (1971). I believe that Winnicott's concept can serve as the basis for a non-reductive psychological framework that illuminates the role of *poiesis* in expressive arts.

If we go back to the origins of psychotherapy in Freud's work, we can see that the actual relationship of analyst and client is neglected in favor of the fantasied relationships of transference and counter-transference. The analyst's attitude towards the patient is one of neutrality, that is, they do not take a role in the patient's internal drama but stays outside in order to let the patient work it through for themselves, using interpretation when appropriate only to show the patient what is behind the symbolic material contained in their dreams and associations. If the analyst is neutral, their interpretations can ultimately show us that what we project onto them is our own fantasy. This insight then, can take the power away from the fantasy and return us to reality.

Freud was very much against the analyst taking an empathic stance toward the patient. In terms of his theoretical framework, this makes perfect sense. If I show myself as too caring, I confuse the desire of the patient with the reality of the analytic situation, for example, by becoming like the "good father" or "good mother" that he always wanted. This would discourage him from projecting onto me the punishing parent that he carries as an internalized part of his psyche (as an over-active and critical superego). In that case, he could not "work through" the fantasy and see it as his own. The same would be the case, of course, if the analyst were to become cold and critical. Neutrality is not uncaring; it is a form of caring which encourages the other to do the therapeutic work on her own. Nevertheless, the actual relationship between the analyst and patient is, one could say, "nothing personal."

Freud's non-relational account of psychoanalysis is based on his conception of the psyche as an independent region of experience, an internal world of feelings and fantasies that originates as a response to the development of the child's biological drives. As the child moves away from a state of biological dependency on the parents, he goes through a conflictual passage to autonomy in which he should be able to satisfy his own needs. The struggle for independence from the authority of the father is then a necessary step in the child's becoming his own person. Neurosis occurs when the passage to adulthood is blocked and the patient is "fixated" at an earlier stage of development.

Freud's theory is profoundly developmental. At the same time, however, it is, we could say, "non-relational," in the sense that the actual relationships within the family are secondary to the internal fantasies of the child, ultimately stemming from his own instinctual development. The goal of development for Freud is autonomy, which he understands to mean independence from the authority of the other. The idea of the autonomous individual is that of a rational being who has mastered his instincts and can satisfy his needs by working upon reality. This is, of course, a traditionally masculine conception of the human being, one which contrasts with the image of femininity as primarily emotional and dependent on others. If we were to play the psychoanalytic game, we could interpret this conception of the autonomous self as a defense against the need for dependency. In any case, it fits the historical tendency of human beings to master the forces of nature for their own benefit, a tendency which has led us to what might be called, in psychoanalytic terms, the "revolt of the repressed," as the domination of nature leads us closer and closer to global disaster.

As psychoanalysis developed after Freud, however, the relational aspect of the therapeutic situation came more into the forefront. We can see this in the development of the object-relations theory of Klein, the precursor of Winnicott's theory and others. For Klein, what is important in the child's development is not only their own drives and desires, but the way in which the child tries to satisfy these needs by incorporating images of others in their family into their own psyche. The child's mind is filled with internalized images of others. These internal images, stemming from their childhood development, are projected onto actual others whom they encounter in the world around them, in particular onto their analyst.

Klein is true to Freud in her emphasis on the biological origins of psychic life. What differentiates her from Freud is her emphasis on the earliest stages of the child's development. Whereas Freud saw the critical stage of development as occurring in the struggle for independence from paternal authority, something which takes place during the period from three to six years, for Klein the most important phase of development comes in the earlier relationship to the mother, in particular to the mother's breast, the primary source of nourishment. Klein also emphasized the death drive, something that Freud theorized much later than he did the drive for love and connection. For Klein, the breast is not only an object which provides nurturance, a "good" breast, but also one that is withholding or intrusive, a "bad" breast. The internal life of the child is thus filled with good and bad objects and with needs for both connection with the good and destruction of the bad. Since these are projected in symbolic form in the child's play, the analyst's role is to interpret the play as a reflection of the child's inner life in the same way as Freud interpreted dreams and associations. Thus Kleinian theory, in spite of its emphasis on the relation with the "object" in the child's development, remains non-relational in its understanding of the therapist–client interaction.

I see Winnicott as initiating the change toward a relational theory of psychotherapy. Winnicott was, of course, within the psychoanalytic tradition in emphasizing the instinctual basis of mental life. Moreover he was strongly influenced by Klein and her development of object relations theory, with its emphasis on the internalized relationship with the mother as the primary factor in development. However, his experience as a pediatrician who saw thousands of children, usually accompanied by their mothers, made it clear to him that the child was always in a real relationship with the mother, not only a fantasy one. In fact, in his view, there is no such thing as a child, in the sense that the child can only be understood in its relationship to its mother. No child exists by itself.

What Winnicott clearly understood was that the relationship with the mother was central to the child's experience and to its self-formation. If the mother is able to respond to the child's needs in a "good-enough" way, i.e., adequately though not perfectly (Winnicott 1971, p.11), the child can develop a sense of trust in itself and in others. It could then be in the world as a "real self," one who expresses its needs directly and trusts that others are there for it. On the other hand, a child whose mother was withholding or intrusive, whose self-preoccupation leads her to respond in terms of her own needs rather than the needs of the child, tends to develop a "false self," one which projects an image of what she thinks her mother wants from her by being, for example, the "good girl" who never causes trouble by insisting on her own satisfaction.

How then does the child's sense of self develop? Here is where the connection of Winnicott's thinking with that of expressive arts therapy becomes clear. For Winnicott, if the mother is able to respond appropriately to the child's needs, the child can feel trusting enough in its own impulses to begin to move away from complete identification with the mother. The way for them to do this is through play. Play is a "back and forth" activity; it requires a relationship with someone or something else. Therefore, for play to take place, the child must first feel safe enough to transition from their identification with the mother. They can then begin to find "objects" other than the mother's body that can be charged with meaning and feeling, for example, the "blankie" or little piece of cloth that so many children get attached to. The child must have this blankie or their sense of being will be threatened. Many parents have learned this at great cost, after they have tried to wash the blankie that is smeared with saliva and dirt or to take it away because it has become so horrible.

These "objects" are what Winnicott calls "transitional objects," since they represent a stage in the development of the child in which they are transitioning from identification with the mother to the development of a separate self. The transitional object is experienced as both me and not-me—it is neither completely identified with (as the mother was during earliest infancy) nor completely separate (as objects will usually be regarded during adulthood). It is therefore "in-between," and to access it I have to enter that transitional space of experience. This is a space that provides comfort and relaxation; it fosters a sense of reverie in which the child can dream and fantasize.

Most important, for our purposes, it is also the space of both therapy and art-making. What is effective in therapy from Winnicott's perspective is not primarily the insights which the therapist provides through interpretation but rather the creation of a space in which the client can dream and set their imagination free, a play-space that both therapist and client participate in. As Winnicott sees it, the role of the therapist is to play with the client or, if the client cannot play, to help bring them into the space of play.

This is a chaotic space in which the separation between client and therapist is put into question. The therapist is no longer the one who is in charge and who understands what is happening. Rather the quest for control and knowledge need to be given up if the therapy is to take place. This transitional space of experience can be confusing and can even lead the therapist who seeks to be in control to experience anxiety. Often, Winnicott believes, therapists try to overcome that anxiety through interpretation. Giving an interpretation can be a way of trying to reassert control and knowledge in a confusing situation. However, the result is that then the play is often shut down. Thus a good therapist must be able to tolerate the anxiety that comes from the chaotic nature of the therapeutic relationship and to trust that something of value will emerge.

A similar situation faces the artist. When encountering the blank page or canvas, the empty stage of a dance or theater performance, the silence that precedes sound-making in music, the artist will experience themself not-knowing what is coming and not being in charge of it. They must therefore "trust the process," i.e., be able to remain in a state of not-knowing and not-being-in-control and to follow what comes to them in the form of image, word, movement or sound in order for the creative act to occur. Only afterwards can they take a step back and reflectively judge whether the result is worthwhile or needs to be revised. Creativity itself, then, needs courage to trust that out of this process something new will be born.

Both therapy and art take place in the transitional space of experience in which the separateness of the ego or "I" is temporarily suspended and a dreamlike state of reverie occurs, a state in which we decenter from our literal reality and enter the alternative world of the imagination. For Winnicott, this transitional space is born in the good-enough relationship with the mother or mothering figure, but sometimes it comes from feeling a lack in this relationship and a consequent need to re-create it anew. If my "real self" has never had a chance to develop, perhaps I can make it come alive through art-making within the context of a therapeutic relationship in which my poietic acts are accepted and validated. Many artists feel most alive when creating, but often this sense of aliveness does not last unless it is contained within a strong relational frame.

Therapeutic effectiveness in this framework, however, does not come primarily from empathy, although this is certainly necessary. Rather, what is most effective in the therapeutic relationship is the creation of a transitional space of experience in which the client can let go of their habitual defenses and re-create themself as if for the first time through play and art-making. Expressive arts therapy, then, can be understood as art-in-relationship—decentering in the presence of the other who can "hold" the client as they enter into the transitional space of creative action.

We all need to feel that our therapist understands us and that they are empathic with our struggles and our suffering, but we also need them to help us let go and find the freedom of imaginative play and art-making. At its best, this is something that expressive arts therapy can provide. The "holding" that is the basis of the therapeutic relationship thus needs to be accompanied by "shaping" so that we can go forward into the future.

Holding and shaping should be understood as two aspects of *poiesis*, the creative act. The therapist needs to be capable of both of these to be effective in their therapeutic work. Thus the relational nature of therapeutic work is essential.

We are always in relationship to others and to the world. Even the act of tearing ourselves away from the world in which we live in order to transform it occurs in relationship to this world. Moreover, through our poietic acts we create new possibilities for others, proposing new ways for us to live together. We need to reject the image of the artist as a solitary genius if we want to understand the essence of *poiesis*. We are in the world as beings-with-others, not as autonomous creatures. Indeed, it is only by acknowledging our essential relatedness that we can find our own individuality.

In expressive arts therapy, then, we seek to form therapeutic relationships that foster *poiesis* as the capacity of a person to respond to others in the world and thereby to find or, we might say, to shape, themselves. Shaping within the session, then, does not only consist in the carrying out of the therapist's aesthetic responsibility but primarily in the client's own creative acts. The therapeutic relationship thus serves to build a poietic capacity that the client can carry into their life outside of therapy. *Poiesis* is essentially relational. We can understand expressive arts therapy only if we put relationship at the center together with art-making.

TO FIDES

I tried to cure myself through therapy
but art was the better way

Sitting alone, writing poems no one would ever see
Are you a writer, she asked, but when I answered,
How did you know?
She just smiled
Later I helped her run away from home

Just kids, Patti says, and when
did we stop being that?
I'm still playing grown-up,
Never so happy as rolling on the floor at Fides,
Lying on my back, my old nemesis
rubbing my feet and the midwife
stroking my hair

Soft song coming from my mouth
Surprise to hear it was beautiful

The world is full of surprise
full of wondrous things
All offstage and out of sight

Give up your upright posture
Lie down and let the world go on its own
The gods come when they will
Though not to those who wait

Soft sounds, voices in the air,
Evanescence

I'll sing to that

3

TOWARDS THE WORK

WINNICOTT, UNINTEGRATION, AND BEYOND

I first encountered Winnicott's writing in the 1970s, when I was training to be a therapist. I liked very much his emphasis on the role of the environment in helping to sustain a healthy sense of self. It seemed to me to be a useful corrective to the exclusive emphasis which many psychoanalytically-oriented thinkers had placed on the internal dynamics of the person. Certainly it resonated with my experience of my own childhood— or at least the story I told myself about it— in which the lack of responsiveness of my family to any attempt to assert my impulses played a major role in my development. One of the ways in which I coped with that non-responsiveness was, as an adult, to search for a community that would welcome me, and that would also welcome others, in our attempts to be ourselves.

Another way was to turn to the arts. For me the arts represented a realm in which I could make something real out of my own subjective strivings and, most importantly, in which the thing made (poem, performance, etc.) could, at least potentially, be received by others. Creativity and community, then, became major themes in my search for myself. At the same time, these themes seemed to resonate with cultural and historical developments, in which many young people rejected the world that was offered to them at the time, a world in which isolation and compliance were seen as the norms for adult living.

One of the themes in Winnicott's writing that seems to be particularly relevant to my experience is that of "unintegration." Winnicott distinguishes this state from the "disintegration" that can happen on both a psychological and political level. As Adam Phillips writes, "Unintegration is a resource, disintegration is a terror" (1988, p.80). For him, the ability to rest in an unintegrated state and to have that accepted by others is key to creative living. Without it, we are consumed by a restless striving that never finds its end.

It was clear to me that this state of unintegration or chaos was something I experienced as a poet and performer. Artistic creation is not possible unless we let go of pre-formed structures and venture forth into the unknown, playing with possibilities in order to let something new arrive. This letting-go is also the source of creative blocks and of performance anxiety, since we have come out of the comfort zone in which we felt safe in order to find unexpected possibilities. Again, the ability to do this depends on there being an other or others who can "hold" us when we start to fall.

In the theoretical framework of the field of expressive arts therapy we call the practice of unintegration "decentering," our name for that phase of a therapy session in which we move away from cognitive control of our experience into a playful exploration with artistic materials, including our own bodies. The one who guides the process of letting-go is responsible for helping clients find the outcome that is just right for them, that "felt sense" we call the "aesthetic response" which is necessary for the process to work.

In this respect, we have moved away from the idea that "the process, not the product, matters," as often stated by arts therapists. The process can be deeply satisfying, of course, but it achieves its goal only in the product that affects the person experiencing it, that touches their "effective reality." This has led us to supplement the role of "play" in expressive arts therapy with a recognition of the importance of the "work." After all, the history of the arts is a history of works that are made. The artist longs for the work to emerge, not just for the experience of art-making. Sometimes this is supremely difficult, at others, it seems to come effortlessly. In any case, the work is the thing that is aimed for. In our framework, we call this a "work-oriented" expressive arts practice.

By emphasizing the work, we move away from all forms of psychological reductionism. We have come to realize that art is not self-expression. The work always brings something new that was not present "inside" the person; it is not something squeezed out like toothpaste from a tube. If we think of genuine works, this becomes clear: Was *War and Peace* "inside" Tolstoy? Were any of his symphonies "inside" Beethoven? This does not mean that art has no psychological significance. On the contrary, the psychological impact of art comes from the works that are made. Who does not recall hearing music or reading a book that gave them the feeling that their lives were changed? Art works, and that is why the work of art is essential.

In thinking thus about the importance of the work, I have moved away from Winnicott's premises. For him, creativity in the therapeutic encounter is all about play. It is reverie or dream, and not something that has a material realization. Of course, Winnicott himself had a great appreciation for works of art. He played music and drew with facility. Yet I do not see in his writing a way to account for the forms that emerge from formlessness, the works that come from play.

Perhaps this has to do with his almost exclusive emphasis on the mother's role in the development of the child, in particular on her capacity to "hold" the infant. This is indeed crucial, and has its counterpart in the therapist's ability to "hold" the client, to provide a safe space for him or her just to be without having to live up to his expectations. But safety is only valuable insofar as it helps us to have the courage to take risks. Something more than maternal holding is necessary at this point. Traditionally this has been the role of the father, as he ushered the child (usually assumed to be the boy) into the world. I am presenting these ideas here in terms of traditional gender roles, as Winnicott did, but the important thing is the principles that these roles embody, the difference between "holding" and "shaping."

The artist's work is to shape the materials. He or she needs to explore them and to let them find their form, but ultimately the artist has the responsibility for the aesthetic outcome. Anyone who has practiced improvisation in theater or other artistic media knows this— we let go to improvise, and then at a certain point we have to guide the process toward a work. Sometimes we need to be ruthless to do this, eliminating our favorite parts for the sake of the total effect. We select, we shape, we revise, and we are not satisfied until it "works."

I suspect that the absence of the father (or what has traditionally been the father's role) in Winnicott's writing is the equivalent of the absence of the work. Personally, I have had to learn the importance of the work at my own peril. I love to play, and sometimes I think I would be content just to fool around forever. But I also think this predilection is in part a reluctance to take a chance and commit to the work. As long as I'm playing with possibilities, I'm safe. Once it's time for the work (and a deadline helps), I need to find the form, and that means giving something up.

I still believe in the primacy of play. Unless we can let go into that primitive state of unintegration, nothing new can possibly emerge. But I see now, after many years of exploration, that the arrival, not just the journey, matters as well. We need to make works, and we need to make a world. Otherwise we doom ourselves to being ineffective, and we let those stay in charge who have no care for the ones under their control.

As I was writing this essay, the Occupy Wall Street and other Occupy events were happening around the world, themselves a sequel to what has been called the Arab Spring. All these events had that improvisatory and playful quality that characterizes the beginning of something new. The participants rightly reject the relevance of the question often posed by outsiders, "But what do they want?" What they wanted is plain enough: an end to the inequality that has grown to intolerable levels in our society.

But the concern that underlies that question, when it is not meant as an accusation, is important: at some point any new social movement has to find its form. Perhaps this form will not be the same as the usual structure of representative democracy, which for the most part is far removed from the living experience of citizens. Perhaps it will embody the playful, participatory quality which has characterized the movement so far. The alternative is not between rigid and lifeless forms of social life on the one hand and pure play and spontaneity on the other. Rather we must find playful forms of life, responsive institutions that can sustain us by honoring our fundamental impulses, political movements that have what I can only call "soul."

Whether in therapy, education, art or political action, we need to live in the paradoxes of work and play, of restful unintegration and effective action. Otherwise we split ourselves off from the world and find ourselves only in an imaginary and ultimately ineffective space.

I come back to the themes of creativity and community. My wish would be to build a playful world together, one in which we can both rest and venture forth. I do not know what shape this world will have, but it will find its form or else vanish like a dream. And if it does become real, only then can we begin to take it apart all over again and build it anew.

ART PARDNERS

We saunter into town,
pens in hand,
ready to write
at the slightest sound.

Watch out!
We're quick on the draw.
Images spring forth
to cover the ground,
flowers among the leaves
of grass.

Watch out!
We'll mow you down.
And next year
we'll bring you back
to life again.

PART II

POIESIS: FROM PHENOMENOLOGY TO IMAGINATION

4

THE FEAST OF IMAGINATION

I wake up in the morning and look at the image that appears in the bathroom mirror. I see that there is dust on my glasses so I clean them. When I go downstairs, the first thing I notice is the cover of a book on the dining room table, *A Cartload of Scrolls: 100 Poems in the Manner of T'ang Dynasty Poet Han Shan*, by James Lenfestey (2007). The cover image, an ink painting on silk, is a reproduction of a sixteenth-century painting of an old man sitting meditatively by the side of a mountain stream. I begin to pay attention to the images around me.

I see the image on the cover of a brochure, *Arts for Global Change: A Program of LTTA*, showing a young Cambodian girl being taught to play the guitar by a Western woman. Her village is visible in the background. I glance at the dining room table and see a page from last Sunday's *The New York Times Magazine*. The page has an image of a pebble used in the "pebble bed" reactor, in which we see the graphite shell of the pebble and a cross-section showing a "speck of enriched uranium" and the "carbon casing." I go to the stove to put on water for tea and see the images on the fridge: A magnet in bright colors depicting a woman holding a palette and joyfully smiling, saying "Art is My Life;" another one of a dog urinating on a "Bush for President" sign; one of a Greek vase; two photographs of my sons, Gabriel and Jesse; one of Paolo Knill, Margot Fuchs, Ellen Levine and myself in a high Alpine setting in Switzerland; an umbrella magnet titled, "*El Paraguas*"; another of a skeleton holding a sickle, "*La Muerte*."

I sit at the dining room table to correct the *POIESIS* journal proofs. On the table is a copy of *The Sun* magazine. The cover image shows an extremely tall ladder reaching to the sky. I correct the pages of Peter Sinapius' article, "The Self is an Image" (2008); and I see a picture of Peter at age five and, on the facing page, one of Malevich's *Black Square*. On the dining room walls, there is a large painting by Ellen of rocks, sea and land, and two by Albert Alcalay: a colored print, *Kafka's Castle*, massive architectural forms looming upward and seeming to advance on the viewer; and an untitled aquatint in gentle colors of a doorway in Jerusalem, done 20 years later. As I start to write this, I look up and see a brightly-colored print by Claire Dolan in the style of the Bread and Puppet Theater: ripe red tomatoes with green stems against a yellow background and the words, "The Right to be Lazy." I am beginning to see images everywhere, a proliferation of images. I am overcome by images.

I look out the kitchen window to my neighbor's house. Is what I see an image or a perception of something real? Even my room starts to seem like an image. I touch my body but do not feel reassured, remembering Dr. Johnson kicking the rock in a futile riposte to Bishop Berkeley's doctrine that to be is to be perceived. Is everything an image? Am I? And you the reader, what image do I have of you as I write or you of me as you read?

Suddenly I understand the iconophobia and iconoclasm of traditional religion, the longing for the Real and the prohibition of images of the divine, as well as Jean-Luc Nancy's reflections on the "forbidden representations" that we are called to make of the concentration camps (Nancy 2005, p.27). In my mind, I paraphrase Theodor Adorno, "To make images after Auschwitz is barbaric" (Adorno 1967, p.34). Yet images are all we have now. They flash across my mind, from Resnais' *Night and Fog* to Spielberg's *Schindler's List*; images of photographs of the survivors emaciated and barely alive; images of the work of Shimon Attie in which he projected visuals of Jewish shops and homes in 1930s Berlin onto the contemporary buildings that have replaced them.

I cannot stop these images from coming. "Lord, deliver me from my imagination," I implore. I, who once so blithely proclaimed, "Power to the imagination!" am overwhelmed by the power of images. I focus on my breathing and search for emptiness, but immediately have an image of a guru instructing me and of myself looking calm and enlightened. I hold on to some lines of Ezra Pound's poetry, even as an image of him as an old man in

St. Elizabeth's hospital who had embraced fascism flickers through my mind. Damn the iconic turn!

I imagine, therefore I do not exist. Can I accept this flux, this fecundity, this dissemination of being? I see an image of myself embracing Dionysus, then see Pentheus as a transvestite spying on the women's rituals, and finally his mother, Agave, proudly bearing his severed head. I close my eyes; but that's worse, the images well up.

"Where is all your postmodernism now, wise guy?" I say to myself. I feel a longing for a simple life in the country (or at least my image of it). Then I notice my breath again and listen to the sounds of the fridge and the noises of the city. I look at the counter and see fruit in a bowl and flowers in a vase. I try to cultivate my love of images rather than allow my fear to cause me to flee them, and I recall James Hillman's injunction, "Stick to the image!" (2015, p.34). I tell myself, "Just look around and see all the amazing images around you, and the memories, associations and ideas they give rise to. Kindly notice them, pay loving attention to them. Look closely at the beauty of the tulips in the vase." As my breath settles down, the fearful images are gone, and I am at peace.

I suddenly realize that the images are a feast, a fiesta, a festival. I look closely at the card made for me by my thirteen-year old friend, Max, in return for a copy of Ferlinghetti's *Poetry as Insurgent Art* (2007) which I gave to him. The card shows a waiter serving dinner. When he takes the cover off the serving dish, a profusion of images rises up: birds, sun, moon, figures of all kinds. Inside the card are the words, "It's like the ambrosia of inspiration on a plate!" I am drunk on the ambrosia of imagination: "For he on honey-dew hath fed/ And drunk the milk of Paradise" (Coleridge 1997, p.250, first published 1812).

SOMETHING TERRIBLE HAS HAPPENED

Something terrible has happened.
I have fallen in love with Peru.
Like all my loves, inappropriate, impossible,
without end.

Not Cuzco. Not Machu Pichu.
Not the myth of an Inca past.
No, the living reality of millions in Lima,
crowding the streets, filling the air
with pollution, with noise.
Faces. Bodies.

Here is the ancient glory,
all madly careening in cars that leave
traces of smoke, cut each other off,
and drive away.

A car from which four young men emerge
to attack a family in a jeep, a family with money
who cut them off,
attacked themselves five minutes later
by four even tougher guys,
chasing them down the road,
smashing their car window,
punching one in the face,
then strutting proudly back like the real Inca warriors,
the bloody history lived today not as myth but as modernity.

Ah, Peru! How can you live?
How alive you are!

And we. Los gringos norteamericanos.
Americans in spite of ourselves
and all our corrections.
We are shielded by our friends
like Latin American dictators
protected from their people.

We eat well. Go to the beach.
Accept the hugs. The admiration.
Leave. And return again.

Ah, Peru, you have stolen my heart!
Cholos! You are here with me in the streets of Toronto.
I see you in the faces of bus riders,
children walking by, all the migrants,
but your soul is in Lima,
in the jungle,
in the Andes.
by the sea.

You hold me captive
with your terrible beauty.
Fierce. Bloody. Alive.

Never set me free.
I say to you again:
Never set me free.

5

IMAGE WORK

IMAGINAL PSYCHOLOGY AND EXPRESSIVE ARTS

In the expressive arts, we often speak of the poetic imagination, the capacity to use the images which arise in the decentering process as the basis for positive change in our lives. I am reminded of the Biblical injunction, "Where there is no vision, the people perish" (Proverbs 29:18). What kind of vision can allow us to respond in an effective way to the challenges we confront? In a world in which images of return to a pristine state of past innocence are put forth as promising happiness and peace, the question arises, how can we conceive of the imagination in a way that will take us forward into the future?

Psychotherapy, for the most part, has not put imagination at the center of its thinking. Psychoanalysis itself begins with an emphasis on memory rather than imagination. For Freud, the analytic cure comes with overcoming the fantasies that compensate for our inability to face the past directly. Only by freeing ourselves from the tyranny of the imagination, for him, will we be able to live meaningful lives. There is very little in Freud's writing that explicitly sees the value of the imagination as a way forward.

This emphasis on memory rather than imagination is maintained in the development of psychotherapeutic thinking, though there are some exceptions. Winnicott in particular sees transitional experience as a state of mind in which the creative imagination is a way toward well-being, but he never develops this into a full-fledged theory. It is not until the work of Jung that the imagination takes center stage. Even then, however, it is subordinated to his emphasis on the process of individuation, the achieving of wholeness. Jung's archetypal images are preconceived as pathways towards the archetype of the Self, the image that represents the integration of all the parts of the person. Images, for Jung, are valued only insofar as they lead to this integration.

James Hillman, a post-Jungian, follows Jung in his valuing of the image, but rejects the idea of an integrated self-hood. Hillman can be considered as a postmodern thinker, in the sense that he dispenses with the idea of a master narrative, a central notion which unifies the diversity of experience under one concept or story. Instead he puts forth a polytheistic psychology that values the fecundity of the imagination, the variety and depth that different images can provide. The expressive arts place a similar emphasis on the value of the imagination. The question then arises, can Hillman's imaginal psychology serve as a foundation for the work of the expressive arts? This essay will address that question.

We have to first ask, what is an image? To use Heidegger's terminology, the image is not something "ready-to hand" (*zuhanden*) that we use, as a hammer might be, nor something merely "present-to hand" (*vorhanden*) that we observe from a distance, like a stone which we might come upon on our daily walk (Heidegger 1962). Rather, the image is a work, something that has been shaped in order to appear to us, to be shown, as a painting is, for example. Moreover the image "works" on us, has an effect, moves us in one way or another. In Greek, the closest term for a work is *ergon*, something which has *energeia* or energy. The image is a work not only because it has been "worked" for the specific purpose of being seen, but also because "it works," i.e., it has *energeia*, a specific charge which is transmitted to us and moves us to action or reflection.

I am writing of the image here in its essential being, and not considering the ways in which we are surrounded by images that are without lasting effect, designed not to be seen in themselves but to be over-looked, to be scanned without pausing and to accumulate without distinction. Such are the images in advertising, on television, on our computers, tablets and cell phones.

Perhaps instead of speaking of the genuine or essential image, we might speak of the poetic image, to use James Hillman's term. In *The Force of Character and the Lasting Life* (1999), a meditation on aging as an opportunity to let who we essentially are emerge more and more clearly to be seen, Hillman speaks of the ways in which old people become "characters," i.e., enter into a condition in which who they are becomes more and more visible. In a sense they become images of themselves, lasting figures whom we will remember when they are gone.

The poetic image is, to my mind, the image in its essential way of being. It is the kind of image that attracts Hillman in his many books and essays, the image that we can contemplate and enter into more and more deeply. Hillman often quotes Jung's sentence, "Image is psyche" (Hillman 1977, p.81). That is, the soul not only experiences images and is drawn to them as its own native land, but it also is an image. All the ways we experience the psyche are imaginal; the imagination is the dwelling place of the soul.

Hillman also likes to quote Keats, who said in a letter, "… the world is a vale of soul-making" (Keats 2012, p.249). For Hillman, the psyche or soul is not something substantial, an underlying and permanent substratum for our experience. Rather, soul is a quality of our experience, it is that which manifests in the experiences that affect us deeply, that, we might say, "animate" us and make us feel alive. What primarily gives us this sense of being and of meaning, for him, is the imagination and the images that it produces or contemplates. We "make soul" through the images that we experience, and specifically through the poetic images. Only these works of the imagination have the power to move us deeply and take us further into our lives.

Since Hillman's thinking does not base itself upon the Jungian notion of wholeness represented by the archetype of the Self, there is no one archetypal image for him that unifies the psyche; rather images are archetypal or poetic when they can animate us and lead us more deeply into the soul. Of course, Hillman still maintains the Jungian tradition of "reading" the image in terms of the myth that contains it, and particularly of using Greek mythology to interpret the images that arise for us in our dreams and other imaginal modes of experience. However, as his thinking "develops," he tends more and more to see the image in its own terms and not as a figure in a larger story, a mythical representative. In *Archetypal Psychology* (Hillman 2015, first published 1981), a short presentation of his basic perspective, he uses the term "archetype" not to name an image which has a mythical resonance but rather as the word for any image which can lead us to soul-making. The archetype is, in fact, the poetic image, the one that takes us from the prose of our life into its poetic depths. This approach is, I believe, more conducive to the practice of expressive arts, with its emphasis on a phenomenological approach to the image. When Hillman says, "Stick to the image" (2015), he is basically abjuring the Jungian framework of interpretation and moving toward a pure phenomenology of the imagination.

Let us return to the question, can Hillman's imaginal psychology serve as a foundation for the practice of expressive arts therapy? In its approach to the image, expressive arts therapy (EXA) attempts to rely on a purely phenomenological method. Instead of interpreting the image in terms of an explanatory framework (Freudian, Jungian, Gestalt or other), EXA engages in an aesthetic analysis, in which the image is asked to speak for itself. The expressive arts practitioner (whether therapist, coach, supervisor or social change agent) helps the client to describe the image in as much detail as possible, by looking closely at its structure and also at the process by which it came into being. At the same time, they ask the client to describe their experience, the sensations, feelings, thoughts and other images that came to them in the process or that arise now. I would say that this is as close to sticking to the image as any reflection can be.

Nevertheless, in the expressive arts, the whole process of image-making (or "decentering," in the language of EXA) is carried out for the purpose of helping the person overcome some difficulty or alleviate some suffering to which they are subject. Thus after the image work that takes place in decentering and the close description of both the process and the product in the aesthetic analysis, a bridge has to be constructed that can help the person return to the life-situation that led them to ask for help.

The "close description" of the aesthetic analysis is one way in which this bridge is built. Another is, as we have said, by asking for a possible title or titles for the work or for the whole process of decentering. This is a way of "crystallizing" the sense of the image. Often the process of aesthetic analysis and its crystallization in a title can lead directly to a meaningful message. This then becomes the bridge to the "harvesting," the phase of the session in which the work of the image is understood in terms of the life problem that was originally discussed in the filling-in.

It is amazing how often this approach works to help a person find a greater range of play. Perhaps there is something in the imagination that is itself liberating, or at least can be if it is guided in a sensitive way. Expressive arts could thus be considered as a "therapy of the imagination" in a double sense: the imagination becomes therapeutic when it is helped to "work" (to educe an "aesthetic response" in the client), and the imagination itself undergoes a therapeutic process, in which it is given space to dream a new reality, one which is not idle daydream or utopian fantasy but is achievable with the resources that are already contained within the person's or group's situation and abilities.

We could say that Hillman's poetic psychology is supportive of the imaginal process of expressive arts contained within an EXA session, insofar as it helps us to consider more closely the role of the imagination in decentering. However, I wonder whether this perspective is sufficient to serve as the basis for the expressive arts understanding of change, whether therapeutic or otherwise. Rather, expressive arts does not stay within the realm of the imagination. Rather, it relies on an implicit conception of the human being as having the capacity to use imagination to bring something new into existence, something which results in a new self-formation and a new relationship to the world.

In other words, to say that psyche is image, then, is to say that human being is essentially "poietic," i.e., that the imagination is the means by which we shape ourselves in shaping the world. This conception of *poiesis* leads us beyond psychology into all aspects of human existence, whether they be social, political, ecological or otherwise. Hillman himself, in despair over the failure of "100 years of psychotherapy" to change the world (1992) has advised us to leave the clinic and the consulting room and deal with the pathology around us. However, it is difficult to see how a purely imaginal psychology can help us to do that. Instead we need a conception of human nature (*Menschenbild*) that takes account of what Merleau-Ponty called the "prose of the world" (1973), the matter (in both senses of the word) with which we have to deal, and also of our capacity to "work" on this material, to use the imagination to transform the world.

We could say that image-work is soul-work, but it is also body-work. In our time we have become more and more aware of this, as the body of the earth comes to appear not as something eternally fixed in form but as something we have made. The challenge for us is not to stay in the psychological realm but to venture forth and engage the world. *Poiesis* does not keep us within the psyche; in that sense, it is not a psychological concept. Rather, it engages our being in the world, whether it is a matter of building a society in which our poietic capacities can help us increase our range of play or of relating to the environment differently, not as natural resource, but as a work that can be the focus of our aesthetic responsibility.

Poiesis, we might say, is image, but only if we understand the image as something that not only works on us, but also as something which confronts us as having been worked and as therefore offering the possibility of being transformed into something new. In expressive arts, the poetic image is valued not primarily as a way of soul-making but as a means of transformation. Beyond archetypal psychology lies the world. We need to change it so that its beauty can shine.

TO HOSSEIN WHO I NEVER KNEW UNTIL NOW

I did not know you, my brother,

Did not see you stopping by the man on the corner,
Slumped over, head hanging in the street

Did not hear you when you spoke to the woman
Lying in the doorway,
Eyes glassy with drug or drink

Did not touch you when you wandered alone,
Waiting waiting waiting
For a word of approval,
For a permit to live without fear

I did not know you, my brother,
In your own country when you were free,
Before you fled to find home

Now I will never know you,
Never see you,
Never hear you,
Never hold you in my arms

All I have are these words to wrap your shroud
And lower you gently into the grave

There the earth will welcome you
And give you the home for which you longed

You are home now, my brother
You are in the ground I walk on,
And I know you at last
Now that you are gone

6

MAN OR BEAST

IMAGINING THE ANIMAL THAT I AM

I am an animal— more or less. I make that qualification in the same words with which I answered the immigration official in Toronto when he asked me, pointing to the woman standing next to me, "Are you married?" Of course he refused to accept my reply. In the eyes of the State, *tertium non datur*; there is no third term between exclusive alternatives. I would have been hard pressed to explain to him that the answer depends on what he meant by "married" or "you" or, even, "are." In the end, I had to answer by choosing one or the other alternative that I was given.

In his book, *The Animal That Therefore I Am* (2008), Jacques Derrida, on the other hand, has no hesitation to name himself an animal, an "animated" creature, we might say, and not only a mind. His words, *l'animal que donc je suis* (the animal that I am), even goes so far as to insert a "*donc*" (therefore) as a challenge to Descartes. *Cogito ergo sum*, "I think therefore I am," said Descartes, when he tried to find a basis for knowledge. When he then went on to ask, "What am I?" and answered, "A thinking thing," he thus effectively excluded the body of the animal from his existence and from the existence of the human as such. This distinction is part of the philosophical tradition, beginning with Aristotle's definition of the human being as *zoon logon echon*—the animal (*zoon*) that has *logos* (speech or reason). Derrida even goes so far as to claim that the distinction between animal and human constitutes the tradition of Western thinking. In following what he writes about the animal, therefore, we are led from the issue of animal rights, a sub-specialty of philosophical thought, into a deconstruction of philosophy itself.

It is indeed a question of following Derrida, who is in turn following the animal. The "*je suis*" of his title means "I am," but it can equally mean, "I follow" ("*suis*" is the first person singular of both *être*, to be, and *suivre*, to follow). When Derrida, therefore, says "I am," he is, at the same time, saying "I follow," and what he follows is the animal. That is, he is on the track of the animal, he is pursuing it (he? she? does the animal have a gender? an important question for him). He is "after" it, in the dual sense of trying to catch it and of coming after it—the animal precedes him; it is in some way his precursor, his abysmal origin which can never be captured or recaptured.

When Derrida says *l'animal que donc je suis*, then, he means he is the animal, more or less. He is the animal but he is also following it and "therefore" is not it, for how can we follow ourselves? However, in another turn or re-turn in his thinking, he is indeed following himself, tracking the traces of the animal in his writings from the beginning. In a retrospective view, he goes so far as to say that the question of the animal has been at the center of his thinking from the beginning, even in his critique of Husserl's phenomenology. For phenomenology ultimately affirms the indubitability of bodily presence, which, in Derrida's eyes, cannot be maintained. To think can never mean to be present; thought turns back, reflects, follows what has preceded—philosophy has known that for a long time (recall Hegel's image of philosophy as the owl of Minerva—another animal—which spreads its wings only at dusk of day). But it is not only thinking that turns back; all life carries traces within it and follows them (if only the traces of the genetic code). Indeed all that exists is not only what it is but what it is no longer; it can never coincide with itself. Identity contains difference (or *différance*, to use Derrida's word) within it. Therefore, as Sartre might say, I am the animal in the mode of not being it. That is, I am an animal, more or less.

When I follow the tracks of the animal that I am, I write the story of my life; I am, therefore, as Derrida says, an autobiographical animal. The conference in Cerisy in 1997 at which Derrida first delivered the seminars in the book was entitled, by his choice, "The Autobiographical Animal." Derrida is an autobiographical animal—as we all are; we all carry the traces of what we are (following), and these traces can be considered to be the original form of "writing."

To follow Derrida, then, I would like to write autobiographically and recall some moments of my own engagement with the animal. Who is the animal that I am (following)? When I was a child, I lived in a world without animals (a state, Derrida says, that we are now in sight of)—not that there were no animals but that I was unaware of any. As I recall (and, like Derrida, I am suspicious of all recollection), none of my friends or relatives had pets. I do not remember a single animal on the streets of Brooklyn where I grew up. My first engagement with an animal came when I was about ten years old. I went to a party, one of my first, wearing new grey flannel pants. When I opened the door to the room, a dog sprang at me and tore a strip of cloth from my pants with its teeth. In my memory, the animal was following me; I was its prey.

My next animal came when I was seventeen and visited the University of Pennsylvania with a friend. Somehow we wandered into a building that housed a number of rooms with animals in cages. The room we entered was presided over by an aging custodian who, for whatever reason, was eager to show us how the animals were being treated. He took a dog from its cage, injected it with a large hypodermic needle, laid it on a metal tray and then slit it from throat to belly. When he pulled back its flesh, we could still see its beating heart. I am haunted by the specter of that animal and by all the laboratory animals that, for whatever reason, "we" have killed. In this case, the animal was the prey.

Predator or prey—*tertium non datur*? A book by Donna Haraway speaks of the human animal as a "companion species," one whose existence depends on the company of another being of a different kind (2003, p.2). In a lecture she gave at The European Graduate School in 2000, the example she spoke about was her dog, and she showed, as I recall, a film of her and the dog kissing, "swapping spit," we used to say. Perhaps the metaphor is appropriate. Red Peter, the humanized ape who delivers the "Report for an Academy," in Kafka's story of that name (2013, first published 1917), (and is recalled by J. M. Coetzee's character Elizabeth Costello in his novella, *The Lives of Animals*, 1999), says that he learned to become human by responding to the sailors who kept him captive and taught him to spit—and to get drunk ("man" therefore, being implicitly defined by Kafka as the spitting, drunken animal, a breach with the philosophical tradition, if not with the actual behavior of philosophers). I have never experienced such a companionship with an animal like the one of which Haraway speaks.

Derrida, on the other hand, refers to his own companion animal (his "familiar," we might say), his cat. As we know, cats are a different species from dogs. They are not primarily for us but for themselves. They regard us from afar, as if our existence were no concern of theirs. When they look at us, we are seen by them. The scene that Derrida recalls (follows) is one in which he is seen by his cat (his "real" cat, he assures us, and not just a figure of speech or thought), and, moreover, seen naked. Seeing the cat seeing him induces in him a feeling of shame, one that leads to a gesture to cover his "private" parts, his sex (and it is only a sexed animal that can induce such shame). He is, we could say, being followed by the animal that he follows.

Derrida's cat (unlike Schrödinger's) was, perhaps, "real," but it becomes a trope for asking who is the animal I am (following). Is the cat "responding" to him; can an animal respond? This question becomes a central one in his interrogation of the tradition; in Derrida's view, the animal is denied that capacity in most philosophical thinking. But there is another related question that he pursues in his pursuit of the animal that is more urgent; it is the one raised by Jeremy Bentham who does not ask, can the animal speak (reason, use tools, have customs, build cultures, etc.), but, does the animal suffer? At once we have stepped aside from the question of thought, a question which differentiates the human from the animal on the basis of a capacity, and moved into the question of suffering, which looks at an in-capacity, a passivity or a passion. The question of who I am (following), then, no longer becomes a question for thinking (in which we reason about the animal), but one for feeling—for even, we might say, fellow feeling, since suffering, vulnerability, mortality, are things we assume in our own existence, things which follow us even as we try to overcome them in and by our thinking (the metaphysics of presence can thus be understood as an attempt to overcome death by denying time and consequently mortality as well).

This same track or trace is followed by Elizabeth Costello in the novella by Coetzee mentioned above. Elizabeth Costello is an Australian writer who has been asked to give a series of lectures at an American university. Her lectures are entitled, "The Philosophers and the Animals," and "The Poets and the Animals." In them she suggests that the philosophers, even those who seek to uphold the "rights" of animals, have failed to understand them; only the poets have been able to do so because only poetic language brings us close to the animal, gives us the animal in its bodily presence. What is more persuasive than her lecture (which remains "philosophical" in its reasoning) is her impassioned statement that she is "wounded" by the suffering of the animal, that it strikes her not in her understanding but, we might say, in her heart. In that sense, we could also say, Elizabeth Costello is "mortally wounded" by the suffering of animals; their suffering affects her in her own mortality. She compares what humans do to animals with what the Nazis did to the Jews, and suggests that our ignorance of what we are doing in our industrial food machines and animal laboratories is a willful ignorance, similar to that of the Germans or others who claimed that they didn't know what was happening in the concentration camps and therefore were innocent of their "inhumanity." Her lectures, however, are tiresome; she hectors her audience and fails to convince them. She is herself tired and old and, we might say, at her wit's end. The lives of animals become more real to her as she herself approaches death.

The Lives of Animals was originally given as a series of lectures by Coetzee at Princeton University and was published under that title. The lectures were subsequently published as chapters (or what Coetzee tellingly called "Lessons") in a later novel, *Elizabeth Costello* (2003). In this book we see not only the familial relationships which color Elizabeth Costello's two "lectures"—already shown in the earlier volume—but also a wider context in which appear other lectures or lessons by Elizabeth Costello, by her sister Blanche (who has now become Sister Bridget) and by a male African novelist. In this plethora of conflicting perspectives, we begin to see that the views of "Elizabeth Costello," the fictional character, cannot be identified with those of J. M. Coetzee, the "real" author of the novel in which she appears. Coetzee makes this clear when Elizabeth Costello, at the end of her life, finds herself "before the gate" (another of Kafka's tropes) and is unable to pass until she tells the judges what she believes. She cannot give them the simple answer that they demand. As a novelist, she says, she is a "secretary of the invisible" (2003, p.199), relaying the words that come to her from without; she has no beliefs of her own. Moreover what she believes at any one moment may be different from what she believes at another; it is not even clear to her who "she" is, let alone what she "believes." Finally, though, under the threat of never passing through the gate to the light beyond ("...strait is the gate, and narrow the way, that leads to life" Matthew 7:14), she affirms that there is one thing she believes in: the "little frogs" in her native country that wait in the mud until the drought is over and can then be "reborn" with the rain (2003, p.217).

When asked by her judges which of the two affirmations of belief or non-belief that she has made are true, Elizabeth Costello replies (responds) that they are really asking, "which is the true Elizabeth Costello: the one who made the first statement or the one who made the second. My answer is, both are true. Both. And neither. *I am an other.*" "You have," she says, "... the wrong person before you. The wrong Elizabeth Costello." The interrogator, like my immigration official, refuses to accept what we might call her "more or less," and insists on asking, "do you speak for yourself?" to which she can only reply, "Yes. No, emphatically no. Yes and no. Both." When she then insists, "I am not confused," he says (turning her words back on her, as all good interrogators do), "Yes, you are not confused. But who is it who is not confused?" At which point, Coetzee writes, the panel of judges "titter like children, then abandon all dignity and howl with laughter" (2003, p.221).

These passages should caution us about the truths that the poets claim to give us (or, perhaps, that philosophers claim the poets give us). Their statements are true—more or less. And the non-identity of the persons who utter these statements, their non-coincidence with themselves, is indeed cause for laughter, especially once we come to realize that it is our own identities that are being spoken of. Existence, we might say, is a joke.

However the matter is not so simple, if it ever was. Elizabeth Costello's ultimate affirmation of belief (her "confession" or credo) is uttered with such passion that we become convinced that she does believe in the frogs (in their "resurrection"), just as we were convinced before that she was wounded by the suffering of animals (their "passion"). There is in fact a disjunction between her pedagogy (her "lessons") and her testimony. We believe her when she testifies, not when she lectures.

Similarly, in *The Animal That Therefore I Am*, there is a disjunction between Derrida's deconstruction of the tradition and his testimony regarding the suffering of animals. In the latter case, we believe him—and here I am not willing to say, "more or less." If he can testify to the passion of the animals rather than to their resurrection, this is perhaps no more than we could expect from one whose thought, as is appropriate to his own tradition, wanders away from its origin and is caught in a perpetual search for its own traces.

Does deconstruction end in an affirmation of belief? Does our "more or less" ever find its appropriate measure? Is there, as my teacher Werner Marx asked in the title of his book, "A Measure on Earth?" (1987). Derrida's trenchant analyses of Descartes, Kant, Levinas, Lacan and Heidegger reveal the problematic nature of the question of the animal (or what Derrida chooses to call "*l'animot*," a made-up word for their singular plurality); his analyses problematize the binary distinction between animal and human that these thinkers maintain, despite their attempt to free themselves from the tradition. But at bottom (in its origin), it seems to me, this "secretary of the invisible" does testify to the suffering of animals and, in so doing, reveals the sympathy that ties us to all living beings. Another name for this sympathy is "love." What else can teach us where the truth lies? And here we come, perhaps, to a sort of resurrection after all. Can we speak not only, as Derrida does elsewhere, of a "democracy-to-come," (2005, p.77), but also of a "life-to-come," a way of living that would include mortality, vulnerability and, yes, animality within it? This would be a resurrection of the body of *l'animot* within time and not beyond it.

What will we say when we are before the gate, as we are in fact right now and at every moment? Will we, at the end of our thought, testify to our belief? And will the panel of animals who are our judges abandon their dignity and howl with laughter? We can only hope that they will show us more sympathy than we have shown them. And we can only hope that at that time we will have found our measure on earth.

SPEAK THE WORD

Work on your alignment
My Butoh teacher said
Well, it's a little late for that
The academic slouch
Or centuries of insignificance
Bowing down before the Lord
Hiding from His wrath

Thou shalt not look upon His face and live
Or say His name out loud
The name a signifier
A holy word

And this flesh?
Too insignificant to matter
Animal being
Unsanctified

Who shall redeem it?
Who shall claim the body parts?
The hair
The teeth
Aligned for transportation

The name alone rising
Smokewards

Ash of the flesh
Redeemed at last

7

THE PHILOSOPHER'S SONG

"In the beginning was the word" (John 1:1). What is it about the voice that makes it seem primary? In *Speech and Phenomena*, Jacques Derrida says that phenomenology, which attempts to look at experience without preconceptions, nevertheless falls prey to the presupposition of the primacy of the voice over the written word (1973). Writing (*écriture*) is understood within this framework to take place at a distance from experience. It is a representation of what is given, whereas the spoken word has an immediate presence which guarantees its claim to truth.

For Derrida, this claim to presence of speech is a metaphysical one that cannot withstand critical examination. Speech is no more immediate than writing; we can never fix the flow of experience by catching it in the web of words. In fact, we could even say that speech is a form of writing, in the sense that it relies on a structure of language which predates it and makes it possible. Immediacy is always mediated; time outruns us all.

The phenomenological claim for the primacy of the spoken word is part of what Derrida calls the "metaphysics of presence" underlying the tradition of Western philosophy since Plato. Derrida sees the task of thinking today to be one of taking apart or deconstructing all philosophical claims to truth to show that they rely on this metaphysical presupposition, which postulates that underlying the flux of time we can find a ground that is stable and unchanging.

Whether phenomenology actually relies on the metaphysics of presence can be debated. What is more interesting for our purposes, however, is the way in which in our daily experience speech does seem to have an immediacy that writing lacks. Walter J. Ong, in *Orality and Literacy* (1982), has argued that the development of writing as a tool for the preservation of speech has brought about a momentous change in our relationship to the world, to each other and to ourselves. No longer is tradition handed down orally by word of mouth. The written word has no need of the bodily presence of the speaker; the immediate relation of self to other is replaced by the mediation of the written text.

Ong's work falls within the context of the school of Marshall McLuhan, in which the supersession of speech by writing is thought to be in the process of being reversed by new forms of electronic media, especially radio and television. Today digital media have created new modes of communication that seem to echo in their immediacy certain features of pre-literate societies. With the development of these new media, there has also been a resurgence of spoken word in performance. The oral tradition is making a comeback; perhaps it never was completely eliminated.

But what about song? Is singing a supplementary mode of speech, one that relies on the spoken word as its ground? Or could we say with the poets that song is the primary phenomenon, not that it is chronologically earlier but that it achieves an intensity of experience that discursive speech can only aspire to?

The ancient "quarrel between poetry and philosophy" that Plato writes about in *The Republic* (1987, p.376) can be re-thought as a debate for primacy between philosophical speech and poetic song. We should remember that the poets were originally singers. In the oral tradition, the word is chanted, if not sung in the way we currently understand singing. And of course, the word "chant" itself comes from the Latin word for song, in the same way as "cantor" means one who sings.

We know that the Homeric epics were chanted by the bards who traveled from court to court. Perhaps all poetry originally took the form of song. Orpheus, the first poet, can be said to have sung the world into being—or at least into a kind of existence in which it comes alive as if for the first time. In the same way, song brings presence to the voice in a way that speech never can.

In the literature about the metaphysics of presence, I have not seen many references to the way in which we use the term "presence" in discussions of theatrical performance. The presence of the actor is the *sine qua non* for an effective performance; we speak about actors as "having presence" or not. Here we come close to one way in which phenomenology's reliance on bodily presence makes sense—there is a difference in the way we experience an actor's performance depending on whether he or she "has" presence.

If this be a metaphysical fancy, so be it. *Ta meta ta phusica* (the title given to the text of Aristotle) originally meant "the one after the one on nature," that is, the untitled text that Aristotle wrote that followed his treatise on the natural world. "After" can also be taken to mean "follow" here; we follow nature by singing the earth. And yet, as Nietzsche himself said about *The Birth of Tragedy*, such a message cannot be authentically written; it can only be sung (1967, p.20, first published in 1872). In the quarrel between philosophy and poetry it looks like the philosopher will always have the last word. But the singer might respond that the philosopher will always be out of tune…

In the beginning is the song.

YOU HAVE TO GO ON A LONELY PATH

You have to go on a lonely path

Walking in silence, attentive
    to sound

Who speaks when all is still

What voice unheard

I seek the place beyond all speech

A song, a cry,

    inarticulate

at the heart

Echo

Mirror

Bell

Time to rise

and sing

PART III

THE WAY OF *POIESIS*: A CHINESE PERSPECTIVE

8

BEAUTY IN EASTERN AND WESTERN THOUGHT

Beauty is a central idea in expressive arts therapy. The aesthetic response, crucial to an effective therapeutic session, is said to arise from an encounter with something that we experience as beautiful. In expressive arts, beauty is experienced as a sensory phenomenon, not as a judgment arising from perfection of form. As Knill puts it, "The response [to beauty] has a bodily origin. When the response is profound and soul-stirring, we describe it as 'moving,' 'touching' or 'breath-taking.'" (Knill *et al.* 2005, p.137).

In Western aesthetic theory, on the other hand, that of Kant in his *Critique of Judgment* (1951, first published 1790), for example, beauty is understood to be a cognitive judgment that we make when the form of a work of art is experienced as a harmonious and complete totality. We can make this judgment only when we are at a distance from the work, when we are "disinterested," that is to say cut off from our daily lives and preoccupations. Further, such a judgment must have the characteristics of universality and objectivity. It is something in which we are not involved, we might say, "personally." Kant's aesthetics is thus consonant with the tendency of Western philosophy to conceive of the thing as an object which stands over and against us and which would be the same for any knowing subject.

What is beauty? Is it, as it is usually understood, even relevant to our practice or do we need to think of it differently to understand its place in our work? From where can we derive such a conception? Do we need to go to a different tradition from the Western one?

These questions occurred to me after reading *This Strange Idea of the Beautiful* (2016), a book by François Jullien, who is both a contemporary French philosopher and a Sinologist who spent years in China studying the classical language, looking at Chinese landscape paintings and familiarizing himself with the writings about them by the Chinese literati over the centuries. Jullien writes with the rare authority of someone who is totally *au courant* with contemporary Western philosophical trends, while at the same time possessing a deep knowledge of the Chinese tradition. He uses that tradition not as an ideal to be emulated but as a vantage point that allows us to look more critically at our own thinking.

Western aesthetic theory begins with a concept of beauty and sees it as the focal point for the whole enterprise of art-making. Chinese classical thought, according to Jullien, does not even have a single term for beauty. In fact, Jullien points out, the translations of Chinese writings about the arts into Western languages take the multiplicity of terms that describe qualities of art-works in Chinese and translate them all into the univocal Western concept of the beautiful.

From a classical Chinese perspective, may beauty even be a "strange" idea? Jullien's radical defamiliarizing of beauty by changing our perspective and looking at it as something questionable, allows us to ask about the ground of beauty. What are the preconceptions that make Western thought put a certain notion of beauty at the center of our thinking about art? What metaphysical standpoint gives rise to our concept of the beautiful, and what role does that concept play in upholding this metaphysics?

For Jullien, the idea of the beautiful arises out of the need for a mediation between the division of the sensible and the intelligible set forth in Plato's work and maintained in the Western philosophical tradition. For Plato, everyday reality is always coming into being and passes away. It is constantly changing and therefore cannot be the basis for truth, for that which is always valid no matter what the circumstances. Plato's favorite examples are the truths of mathematics, especially geometry. The properties of the circle are always the same, no matter when, where or by whom they are calculated. In fact, the circle cannot be found in our sensible world. It is a purely intelligible concept, without determinate size. In Plato's thinking, the same is true for morality; the good is always the same, though particular instances of it may vary.

If, then, there is a gulf between what is revealed to us by the senses and what is grasped by the intellect, we need a mediator to bring them together. The beautiful fulfills this role, since at one and the same time it is shown to us in each beautiful thing and yet also is the idea by which we judge those things to be beautiful. Thus Western thought isolates and abstracts the beautiful and then uses it as the criterion to judge whether anything in particular fits this criterion. The question then arises, to what extent does this particular thing resemble the beautiful itself?

Moreover, the beautiful shows itself as form, that which stands out before us in a clear and distinct way. Only that which has a harmonious form in which all the parts are coordinated can be thought to be beautiful. The lack of harmony, then, will result in the object being judged ugly. The model for Western aesthetics is the nude, the human body which is perfectly proportioned. The form of the naked body becomes the ideal for art. It resembles as far as possible the beautiful.

What then is the case in classical Chinese thinking about the arts? First of all, Jullien cautions us, we must not take contemporary writing about the arts in Chinese to be definitive. In fact, he says, Chinese thinkers have themselves adapted the Western idea of the beautiful and reinterpreted the art of the classical period in these terms.

Jullien, on the other hand, has gone back to the conversations about painting between Chinese literati during the classical period and found that there is no univocal concept of the beautiful. Rather, the qualities of painting are described in a variety of ways, many of which are in tension with one another. What holds these polarities together is the "yin and yang from which the engendering of the world follows" (2016, p.33), as each member of the polarity yields to the other.

The archetypical instance of this opposition is not the nude but the landscape, the play of mountain and water in which the viewer can be absorbed. The landscape does not present itself to us as an object that we can capture by our gaze. Rather, the landscape absorbs us. It allows us to become lost in it, to wander from peak to vale without fixing our gaze upon a determinate object.

The landscape in classical Chinese painting takes us in, it invites us to linger endlessly without coming to a terminus. Above all, it is not an object from which we are separated and which we, as autonomous subjects, can grasp. The landscape does not reveal being to us, but rather is permeated by life (*chi*), a process full of significance, which can never be exhausted.

Thus, in a way, we can say that there is no such thing as Chinese aesthetics, i.e., in the sense that aesthetics has come to mean for us the science of beauty. Rather, the conversations of the literati about landscape painting meander. They are opportunities for intimacy in being together, nothing more.

Moreover, Jullien points out, the recent development of painting in the West has itself deviated more and more from the ideal of the beautiful object. Rather, Western art now focuses on the construction of the work, the process which brings it into being. We become more interested in what the artist is doing than in what he has made. The goal even becomes that of a continuous process in which the work is never finished. Art itself, for us, has left the idea of the beautiful behind.

Nevertheless, Jullien points out, beauty does not die so easily. When we are confronted, to use his examples, with the nude or with Venice, we can only stand back and say, "How beautiful!" The beautiful has become indispensable for us. Moreover, the thought of the beautiful is something that is available to all of us. In Kant's philosophy, which is the culmination of Western aesthetic thought, beauty is revealed to us through our common sense, it touches us in our humanity. Thus the beautiful opens up the possibility of a public and leads us to the formation of a democratic space, something, Jullien thinks, that was not available in classical China.

Thus, after thoroughly deconstructing the beautiful, Jullien tells us that "we can no longer believe in it nor can we do without it" (2016, p. 248). Rather we need to "reflect upon what an adventurous idea it has been" (2016, p. 251), to probe its preconceptions and to see what paths it still opens up for us. Standing within the tradition of Chinese landscape painting enables us to see the beautiful as "strange," not in order to Orientalize ourselves, an impossible task even for the Chinese, but in order to open up new possibilities not only for the arts but for our culture as a whole. Above all, Chinese thinking about landscape painting tells us that there is another way than that of Being (as Emmanuel Levinas entitled one of his books on the encounter with the Other, *Otherwise than Being*, 1998)

What, then, happens when we look at the use of the arts in therapy? Perhaps we find many things we already knew but did not know how to account for. The work of our clients does not aim at beauty in the classical sense but at life. It is often chaotic and unfinished. It does not distance itself from us, but rather draws us in and affects us emotionally. Above all, it is in process—the experience of making it opens us up to a creative way of living, not to a finished state of being, as Shaun McNiff never ceases reminding us (1998).

Moreover, the arts in therapy are relational—they happen between the therapist and the client. Sometimes they are the product of the joint work of the two, but in any case they can only be understood as occurring in the "intermediate zone" to which D. W. Winnicott refers (1971, p.123). We require a "relational aesthetic," to use the phrase of Catherine Hyland Moon (2002, p.131), in order to understand therapeutic art.

What then of beauty? Is it of no use to us in understanding the arts in therapy? I think it is, as beauty can still be employed in discussing contemporary art. In a play-oriented decentering phase of an expressive arts session there is no end product aimed at but a continuous back and forth, which delights in its own process. We must remember, however, that the tradition of the arts on which we stand leads to the making of a work—the painter wants the image, the poet wants the poem. They are not satisfied with the making alone but aim for the thing made. Art may begin in play, in improvisation and exploration, but it is necessary, as H.G. Gadamer writes, for play to transform into a structure for a work to emerge that can be identified and repeated, albeit differently each time (2004, p.101). Even in the therapeutic process, it is possible for a playful exploration in sound or movement, for example, to be repeated and shaped into a song or a dance that evokes what we have called an "aesthetic response" for the client, not a disinterested and detached judgment of beauty but a felt sense that "takes the breath away" and "touches" us.

In this sense, beauty still has a place, but it is a different kind of beauty, not the disinterested judgment of resemblance to the Idea but the felt sense of a living presence that matters to the artist and the viewer. Perhaps we can say it is a "living beauty," one that through its disparateness and chaos carries the energy of life. It is a beauty that is unfinished, that carries on in the work and in the life. It is neither the isolated and abstract beauty of the West (i.e., Europe) nor the meditative process of the East (i.e., classical China), but something still arriving, in the way that Derrida speaks of the "democracy-to-come" (2005, p.77).

It is not surprising that Jullien is able to undertake his philosophical critique of beauty as the linchpin of Western metaphysics, since all of postmodern thinking is based on a critique of the subject-object opposition that underlies that tradition. Not only deconstructionism but also other trends in philosophy and psychology have the same basis. What Jullien's informed comparative perspective does, though, is to give us an "outside" that enables us to see the "inside" more clearly. Suddenly our own perspective looks "strange" to us and motivates us to go beyond it to a new point of view.

What that point of view will be is not yet clear. Perhaps it will never become clear, as clarity is only a virtue for a standpoint that is not involved in what it sees. For us, on the other hand, as our work in the arts therapies shows us, there is an area of experience that is inchoate, even muddled, but that is pregnant with meaning and with new possibilities to come. Perhaps it is our responsibility to open a space for what is coming, the "rough beast" to use Yeats' phrase, who this time may bring us joy rather than destruction (1959, p.185).

This intermediate area of experience, in which we are not faced with an object opposed to us which we can survey, nor are we in the autonomous position of the subject who can master this object, depends on our willingness to give up knowledge and control. Here perhaps is where we can learn from the Chinese masters, particularly in the Taoist tradition, as we indicate in the following essay in this book. If we can follow what is emerging, instead of dominating it and forcing it to go our way, then something new may emerge which we had not envisaged beforehand. This is indeed the way of the artist, as well as that of the sage.

"Giving up control in order to achieve mastery," as Paolo Knill often says, is to follow the path of *wu-wei*, "non-action," in the sense not of doing nothing but rather of letting our own acts follow the path of what is happening, joining it and helping it to find its own way. This may be the only attitude which can lead us to the "living beauty" that goes beyond the opposition of East and West.

THE BEAUTY OF FLOWERS

The beauty of flowers
Is a beauty of endings

If it lasted,
Who could stand it?

Let it die
Oh, let it die

9

THE TAO OF *POIESIS*

CHINESE PHILOSOPHY AND EXPRESSIVE ARTS

Chuang Tzu, the great Taoist thinker, once wrote, "The cavity of the body is a many-storied vault; the mind has its Heavenly wanderings... If the mind does not have its Heavenly wanderings, then the six apertures of sensation will defeat each other" (1964, p.138). In a similar way, Henry David Thoreau, the great American naturalist, gave a fanciful etymological derivation of the English word "saunter" in his essay, "Walking" (2013, first published 1862). To saunter means to walk without aim or purpose, in other words, to wander. According to Thoreau, the word derives from the French. In the Middle Ages, crusading knights on their way to Jerusalem were said to be going *à la saint-terre* (to the holy land). "Children," Thoreau writes, spying wandering beggars, would exclaim, "'There goes a Sainte-Terrer,' a Saunterer, a Holy-Lander" (2013, p.1). To saunter or wander aimlessly is, then, to be engaged in a holy act.

The knights, of course, had a goal in mind: to liberate Jerusalem from the infidels. This could only be done by the sword. For them, violence was the way to sanctity. It is no accident that Thoreau was not only a great naturalist, living alone for a time on Walden Pond and limiting his needs to the bare minimum, but also an apostle of non-violence, protesting the American war against Mexico and the expansion of slavery into the Southwest by going to jail for refusing to pay his taxes. In fact, Gandhi may be thought to derive his philosophy of non-violence from Thoreau's notion of civil disobedience.

One might well ask, is goal-directed activity necessarily violent? Does action directed to achieving a purpose have to involve force? Is there another Way (Tao)? These questions go to the heart of Taoism and to that of expressive arts (EXA) as well.

The possibility for the arts to be used in the helping professions is based on *poiesis*, decentering from the difficulty and entering the alternative world of the imagination as a means of transforming the situation in which the individual or group finds itself. How, then, can we understand the practice of *poiesis* in expressive arts?

Poiesis in this sense goes beyond the instrumental understanding that is directed toward a specific goal. Imaginative engagement requires a letting-go of "end-gaming" and a willingness to explore whatever may come. It requires a giving-up of control and a willingness to "let something be." In this sense, decentering is similar to what is called in Taoism *wu-wei*, the not-doing that is the essence of Taoist practice. To understand this similarity, it may prove helpful to compare the philosophical foundations of Taoism with those of the expressive arts.

What, then, is the relationship between the Tao and *poiesis*? Is there a hidden affinity between *wu-wei* (non-action) and the EXA practice of "decentering?" These questions will be explored by wandering in the two different realms of Taoist philosophy and the expressive arts on a voyage of discovery. The practice of expressive arts in therapy and its theoretical framework as developed will also be outlined.

Taoism is often understood as a specifically Chinese mode of thought in sharp distinction from Western philosophy. The dominant tendency in Western philosophical thinking takes for granted the purposeful nature of life and of the thinking required to do justice to it. The very structure of philosophical reasoning resembles that of a forceful march through intellectual territory, conquering an opponent by marshaling one's arguments in order to achieve logical consistency as defined by the principle of non-contradiction—a method that is radically different from the paradoxical expressions of Taoist thought, especially those of Lao Tzu.

In the Platonic dialogues, Socrates engages in combat with his interlocutors in order to demonstrate the inconsistencies in what they claim to know. And in *The Republic*, the great text of classical political thought, the just society is envisioned as protected by guardians, soldiers who embody the spirit of the city, in the same way as the *thymos*, the spirited part of the soul, is said to be the location of courage and passion, that which drives a person to action. The only class of citizens higher in rank than the guardians are the philosophers, who rule over all by virtue of their knowledge of what is true and therefore best for others.

This conception of philosophy is a far cry from the account of Socrates' own quest for knowledge, as reported in Plato's *Apology*. Chaerophon, a friend of Socrates, asked the oracle of Delphi (traditionally thought to be able to enter into trance in order to serve as the mouthpiece of the gods), was there anyone wiser than Socrates in Greece? When Socrates was told that "The priestess replied that there was no one," he only became confused, since he was well aware of his own ignorance. The only conclusion that he could come to was that he alone of all those whom he had questioned was aware that he did not know. The philosopher, then, was not to be understood as one who possessed knowledge, as the Sophists, itinerant teachers of rhetoric and public speaking, claimed to be, but rather as one who loved wisdom and, in his ignorance, pursued her wherever he could.

This seems quite different from the conception of the philosopher-ruler in *The Republic*, one who knows the truth and acts in accordance with it; yet the seeds of the Platonic conception are already contained in the Socratic method. By demanding that those who claim to know provide a consistent and principled explanation of their supposed knowledge, Socrates implicitly assumed that the truth is founded on non-contradiction. Only statements that possess logical coherence can lay claim to truth. If we compare this with the paradoxical utterances of the *Tao Te Ching*, we can see a fundamental difference between Platonic philosophy and Taoism. As the first sentences of the Chinese text are sometimes translated, "Those who know do not speak. Those who speak do not know," or in Arthur Waley's classic translation, "The Way that can be told of is not an Unvarying Way; The names that can be named are not unvarying names" (1958, p.141). We can imagine what a Taoist would think of Plato's *Republic*, where the philosophers rule by their claim to knowledge of an unchanging ultimate reality.

Why such wandering in the realms of ancient Greek thought? For one thing, the whole of Western philosophy, as Alfred North

Whitehead has remarked, can be seen as a series of footnotes to Plato (1979, p.39). But not only has Plato's concept of the supremacy of rigorous knowledge been dominant in the West, his placing of poetry and the arts outside the sphere of truth has also been taken for granted. In *The Republic*, the poets are to be exiled from the just city, since in Plato's view, their stories are riddled with inconsistencies and can lay no claim to the constancy of truth. They only serve to disturb the people and keep them from sticking to their appointed tasks. *Poiesis*, then, the making of works that are to be seen or heard, is understood to be radically different from *philosophia*, the knowledge of that which transcends the shifting images provided by the senses. For Plato, science and art are to be distinguished as truth from falsehood.

This denigration of *poiesis* is a rejection of the traditional transmission of knowledge in classical Greece through stories told in epic and tragedy. *Mythos* is to be replaced by *logos*, story by reason. In fact, the story is the archetypal mode of wandering, as the storyteller himself goes from city to city telling his tale to those who rule. In a way, all stories can be said to descend from the *Odyssey*, that epic account of the wanderings of Odysseus who leaves his home and goes from adventure to adventure without arriving at any other destination than that of returning to where he began. Philosophers, on the other hand, do not wander; they stick to their posts.

Wandering, *yu*, is the way or Way (Tao) in which the Taoist Sage proceeds. Instead of laying down principles derived logically from an ultimate truth, he tells stories that show how non-knowing can liberate us from the narrowness of our conceptions. In the Greek language, a principle is an *arche*, and the prince or ruler is the *archon*. Just as the prince rules over the people, the principle dominates empirical reality. There is a certain tyranny implicit in the formation of concepts that aim to comprehend the wealth of experience by abstraction, a process that can only impoverish our lives. How much more pleasant, Chuang Tzu might say, to wander in the cloud of unknowing and to rest in the boundless.

If there were endless space for this essay, we could wander further in the history of philosophy and show the counter-trends in Western thought to the Platonic concept of knowledge. In fact, Plato himself could never overcome *poiesis*. In the Platonic dialogues, the dominance of reason is presented in the form of dramatic conversations, ultimate truth is only to be conveyed by metaphor, and a mythical account of the afterlife is provided as a guarantee of the truth of Socrates' thinking—all of these, of course, are modes of *poiesis*.

Moreover, contemporary Western thought, faced with the destructive impact of the blind application of scientific knowledge to technology in a quest to dominate nature, has re-discovered the cognitive value of *poiesis*, seeking in the divagations of the imagination an antidote to the imperial tyranny of the Idea. Nietzsche, in opposition to the arid dominance of Apollonian logic, appeals to the Dionysian rapture conveyed by Greek tragedy to bring a new birth to the spirit of music (1967). And Heidegger, rejecting the theory of truth as the correspondence of statements to what is already present, envisions truth as the uncovering of what is hidden and *poiesis* as the primary mode of this uncovering (2002, first published 1950).

Poiesis is the Way (Tao) of expressive arts, a way of wandering, sauntering—"erring," in the old English sense of the word, going off the beaten track. In the Middle Ages, in addition to crusading knights on their way to conquer the infidel, there were "knights errant," those who had lost their patrons and were forced to wander the countryside in search of sustenance. For Heidegger, wandering becomes a way of thinking, to the point where he entitled one of his books, *Holzwege* ("forest-paths"—trails in the woods that lead nowhere), published in English as *Off the Beaten Track* (2002). Only by not-knowing, then, can we discover that which is hidden and which reveals itself as a surprise.

However, for this way or method to make sense, it is important that *poiesis* be understood differently than it is usually conceived of in the tradition of Western thought. Under the dominance of the instrumental conception of knowledge, creative action is usually understood as a form of goal-directed behavior. The artist is said to have an idea in his mind and then to impose it upon his material, much the same way as the creator-God has formed the world. Obviously, if this is the case, then *poiesis* cannot result in anything new, it is only the reproduction of the original idea in a different form. Such a conception often underlies the practice of interpretation in the arts therapies. Art is then understood as self-expression, as the outward manifestation of an inner state of mind, and the work of art is interpreted as a reflection of a pre-existing mental state that is subject to diagnosis.

The practice of *poiesis*, however, shows us that, whatever the initial idea, feeling or sensation, the image has a mind of its own, taking us into new and unexpected paths. The role of the artist is to follow the image, not to impose a pre-conceived plan, no matter how good it may seem to be. Imagination, we could say, is a cloud-based activity, urging us to let go of our goal and ride upon the wind. It is true that the work of art is expressive, but art-making is not self-expression. The work expresses, not the self. This is the lesson that expressive arts practitioners have learned from basing their practice on *poiesis* rather than psychology. In opposition to psychological explanations based on pre-existing formulations, the expressive arts uses a phenomenological method, paying close attention to what shows itself and letting it tell us what its meaning is, rather than telling it what we think it means.

Here is where the convergence of expressive arts with Taoism is most evident. *Poiesis* is not the imposition of an idea on inert material; rather it is a form of *wu-wei*, "non-doing"—activity without force or violence that lets itself be guided by what emerges, following it no matter where it may take us to wander. The term *wu-wei* "describes a state of personal harmony in which actions flow freely and instantly from one's spontaneous inclinations… and yet nonetheless accord with the situation at hand" (Slingerland 2000, p.300). If there is a kind of mastery that results from this ability, it is not control over the other but precisely the letting-go of control. We may even say that true mastery comes from the letting-go of control.

The artistic process does involve conscious shaping on the part of the artist, in the same way that the work of the therapist involves not only receptive listening but also intervening to help the client find his way. However, this shaping is more of a guiding than an imposing, part of the "aesthetic responsibility" of the companion. It does not require artistic expertise in a particular medium but rather the capacity of "low skill/high sensitivity," that is, being sensitive to what is emerging and ready to follow it wherever it goes. If there is skill involved, it is in the mastery of the guiding process. Guiding implies the ability to get lost without falling into a desperate attempt to find one's way again. It is similar to John Keats' concept of "Negative Capability," the essential quality of the poet, which occurs "when a man is capable of being in uncertainties, mysteries, doubts, without any irritable reaching after fact and reason" (1899, p.277). The shaping process demands this ability to be "comfortably confused," as Paolo Knill likes to advise students, until a way appears that one can follow.

Similarly, the clown classes that Ellen Levine and I teach to students training to be expressive arts therapists always begin with what is called the "nothing turn." A "turn" in clown involves getting up in front of an audience and performing in some way, but a "nothing turn" is when the clown stands in front of others without doing anything, that is, not trying to amuse but just being there. This is much harder than one might think. Doing nothing does not mean being rigidly still; it implies the capacity to be present in the moment, to be fully alive without effortful striving. From this place of aliveness, all kinds of activity can emerge, and the poetic essence of the clown can show itself in a genuine way. In a similar manner, the expressive arts therapist must let go of trying to help the other person by directing them to a goal and, instead, be fully present with them by giving the gift of his own presence (Atkins and Eberhart 2014). Then the correct path to follow will appear of its own accord.

Not-doing is a way of becoming present, of returning to what is called in Taoism the "Uncarved Block," *pu*, the primal condition of being without form. From this place of pure potentiality, anything can happen. By being present without aiming at a goal, the guide can help clients find their own Uncarved Block and "get out of their own way." Becoming fully present and returning to the Uncarved Block does not imply passivity. The guide acts, but she does not strive.

Chuang Tzu tells the story of Cook Ting, who

> *was cutting up an ox for Lord Wen-hui. At every touch of his hand, every heave of his shoulder, every move of his feet, every thrust of his knee—zip! zoop! He slithered the knife along with a zing, and all was in perfect rhythm, as though he were performing the dance of*

the Mulberry Grove or keeping time to the Ching-shou music. Lord Wen-hui marveled at this and exclaimed, "Imagine skill reaching such heights!" To which Cook Ting replied, "What I care about is the Way, which goes beyond skill... I go at it by spirit and don't look with my eyes. Perception and understanding have come to a stop and spirit moves where it wants." (1964, p.46–47)

Wu-wei is effortless activity. It requires letting go of striving after a goal, and instead paying close attention to what is happening. Then action can happen of its own accord, as if it were unfolding by itself. In writing a poem or making music, the poet or musician must first of all listen for the words or sounds that are emerging and only afterwards bring his critical faculties to bear in a process of revision. The expressive arts therapist acts in an "art-analogue" way, by putting aside diagnoses and treatment plans and instead paying careful attention to what is emerging, intervening only to facilitate the process. This may require multiple "takes" or rehearsals on the part of the client, following suggestions by the therapist for ways to act that will allow the process to find its own way and, in so doing, achieve an "aesthetic response" that brings a sense of completion. The paradox of *wu-wei* in therapy or art is that the desired result is to be attained only by giving up all attempts to reach it. It is to let go and "trust the process," as the title of Shaun McNiff's book tells us (1998), but in doing so, to arrive after all at the goal of healing through the experience of beauty.

This way runs counter to our normal mode of behavior. To engage in *wu-wei* or *poiesis* is to follow a road not taken, to wander off the beaten path into undiscovered territory. It is to take the low road, to enter the valley and to give up the ambition of scaling the heights. This process also means letting go of knowledge and control, the two functions of the ego, as Freud characterizes it, that allow us to survive in the world. The very notion of the deity as omniscient and omnipotent shows the significance of these two activities of the mind. Not only is *wu-wei* foreign to the dominant tradition of Western thought, but the survival mechanisms of the human organism itself lead us to experience non-action as in opposition to our continued well-being. Therefore, a deliberate "step-back" must be taken, a refraining that runs counter to our impulses, in order to activate the potency of *wu-wei*. In French, we say *"reculer pour mieux sauter,"* to step back in order to leap forward. And it is indeed a leap in the dark that we must undertake in order to make things evident that were previously hidden.

By taking this leap, we land in what Po Chü I calls "Not-Even-Anything Land" (Chuang Tzu 1964, p.vii). This is the world of the imagination, where anything can happen and where nothing is fixed or final. Victor Turner calls it a "liminal" or "in-between" space, taking the term from the phase of ritual in which transformation happens by temporarily giving up one's place in the social structure in order to return with a new and renewed sense of identity (Turner 1995). For D. W. Winnicott, as we have noted, this is the space of transitional experience, in which the infant is in-between identifying with the mother and becoming a separate individual, a space where creativity flourishes. In Winnicott's view, adult creativity is achieved by temporarily stepping away from purposeful activity and entering the transitional space again (Winnicott 1974, first published 1971).

In expressive arts therapy, the therapist "decenters" from the literal reality of the person or group and helps them to enter the alternative world of the imagination (Knill *et al.* 2005). This is the world of *poiesis*, where new images and symbols can emerge that point the way to previously undiscovered possibilities. To be in this world requires a process marked by "flow," in which we let things happen and follow them "without any irritable reaching after fact and reason." (Keats 1899, p.277). This is indeed the process of *poiesis*, the world of poetic (or, we might say, "poietic") experience.

Moreover it is not only the "process" of *poiesis* that reveals truth, it is also the "product" or work that emerges that enables us to discover what we did not know. For Heidegger, *poiesis* sets the truth into a work. It results in a structure (*Gestalt*) that can hold the tension between uncovering and concealing, what Heidegger calls "World" and "Earth" respectively (2002). This means that the work shows the truth, bringing it into the light, but also that there is always something concealed in this uncovering. The mystery can never be completely disclosed and remains to be pursued.

Nevertheless, the authentic work affects us; it has an energy that moves us in some way. As we have noted, the Greek word for energy is *energeia*, and a work is called an *ergon*. *Energeia* is sometimes thought of as "power in action"; the work manifests this power in its impact on the maker. In this sense, expressive arts therapists disagree with the customary maxim of the arts therapies, "It's the process, not the product." This slogan is designed to set non-artists at ease, but it neglects the very essence of art-making. Certainly the process is essential, but the artist wants the art-work, not only the experience of making it.

Energeia can be thought of as similar to the Taoist notion of *ch'i*, the breath or life force that animates beings. In African-American culture, an equivalent word for *ch'i* might be "soul." If a work or a practice does not embody soul, it has no power to move us. It is lifeless and inert; it bores us to tears. The art-work that emerges in expressive arts therapy must have *ch'i* to affect us through an encounter with beauty.

We know when beauty is present by our "aesthetic response" to it, the bodily-affective experience of being "moved" or "touched." In an expressive arts session, the aesthetic response of the client tells us that the work has had an effect upon him. We call this his "effective reality," in analogy to H.G. Gadamer's concept of "historical reality," that aspect of history that is particularly meaningful for our own situation, in contradistinction to the vast expanse of meaningless historical facts (2004). It is the "aesthetic responsibility" of the therapist to help the client have an aesthetic response, by means of making a work that brings an experience of beauty.

In this process, the important thing is to set a challenge that the client can meet through her own capacities. The purpose of *poiesis* in expressive arts practice, a purpose achieved only by "letting go of the outcome," is to help clients contact the resources that they already bear within themselves. Expressive arts therapy is thus a "resource-based" practice that aims to help those with whom we work become aware of their own capabilities, an awareness that can be carried over into their literal reality so as to be better able to respond to their own difficulties.

Poiesis can be said to evoke the power of *te*, that innate quality that beings manifest by following the Tao. Expressive arts relies on the conception of human beings as essentially "poietic," that is, as entities capable of shaping their lives in accordance with their own possibilities—in other words, being able to manifest their own *te* by following the Tao. Shaping here does not imply the capacity to make the world or the self however we like. We are not creator-gods with unlimited power. However, we can always respond to what is given, and in this sense we are free to make our worlds and ourselves anew.

The work of *poiesis* never comes to an end. We cannot know or reveal the ultimate truth about the world or about ourselves; therefore, shaping will never be complete. Rather than cause for dismay, however, the recognition of the limits of our knowledge and action sets us free for an endless search, a wandering farther and farther from home. What could be more pleasant than to wander endlessly in the realm of *poiesis*? Such is the power (*te*) of the Way (Tao). Its endless productive capacity is an occasion for wonder, not dismay.

If all roads ultimately lead to home, then let us set forth on our wandering way and marvel at what lies still ahead. The Tao has no end, and only by letting ourselves get lost will we ever come home to tell the tale.

In his essay on walking, Thoreau says:

> *They who never go to the holy land in their walks, as they pretend, are indeed mere idlers and vagabonds, but they who do go there are saunterers in the good sense... So we saunter toward the Holy Land; till one day the sun shall shine more brightly than ever he has done, shall perchance shine into our minds and hearts, and light up our whole lives with a great awakening light, so warm and serene and golden as on a bank-side in Autumn. (2013, p.1)*

And there we shall rest—until we set forth once more.

> *Leaving homeland, parted from kin, banished to a strange place,*
> *I wonder my heart feels so little anguish and pain.*
> *Consulting Chuang Tzu, I find where I belong:*
> *surely my home is there in Not-Even-Anything land.*

Po Chü-I (*Chuang Tzu*, p.vii)

PART IV

POIESIS, IMPROVISATION, IDENTITY

10

EXPECTING THE UNEXPECTED

THE WAY OF IMPROVISATION

When we think about understanding something, we usually have in mind something that has already happened. We are engaged in a backward glance, looking again at what has been in order to comprehend its significance. Hegel spoke of philosophy as the owl of Minerva, which takes flight only at the close of day (Minerva or Athena in Greek is the image of wisdom). The same is true of psychotherapy, which usually seeks to comprehend the self by studying its origins in the past.

Improvisation, on the other hand, indicates action that looks forward to what has not yet been and cannot be anticipated—the *imprévu*, that which cannot be seen in advance. How then can improvisation become a method for understanding? How can the unknown show us the way forward?

Perhaps we can find a clue to this dilemma by looking at improvisation in the arts. In a sense, all art-making has an improvisational element—it aims to bring something new and unforeseen into being. Even works produced according to classical models give us a new way of seeing what is old. However it is not until the advent of modernism that the new became the explicit goal of making art.

In part, this quest for the new is a consequence of the breakdown of tradition. In a period of rapid technological and social change, the rules according to which we act come into question. If traditional models can no longer be relied upon, then we must operate as if we were starting all over again. Improvisation is usually thought of as an erasure of the past, action in which at every moment something absolutely new is brought into being. The logical conclusion of this would be "free improvisation," art-making that is based on no agreed-upon form but creates the very rules that it follows.

In this essay, I would like to explore the idea of improvisation by reflecting on my own experience in artistic improvisation. I will then look briefly at the role of improvisation in expressive arts therapy and research by discussing the dissertation of Sabine Silberberg, a colleague and former student.

My own experience as a performing artist has been primarily in improvisational styles, including Lecoq-based physical theatre (clown, neutral mask, bouffon, *commedia dell'arte*), improvised vocal expression in the Roy Hart tradition, and Butoh (Japanese postmodern dance). It is interesting to see what happens when highly-skilled professional performers come to workshops in these improvisational methods. They have much greater difficulty finding their way than do amateurs such as myself, since their established technique often inhibits them from discovering something completely new.

Of course, much of what happens in improvisational classes and workshops is not very good art. Participants may enjoy themselves by engaging in free expression, but the results are usually of little interest to the audience. The main problem in improvisation is that the performer gets in her own way—her subjectivity becomes the content of the work. Art is then used as a means of self-expression.

In my experience, on the other hand, I have seen that self-expression is the death of art. As my Butoh teacher, Denise Fujiwara, says in her classes (quoting her teacher Hijikata), "The first rule of Butoh is, 'Kill the self!'" She goes on to say, "The second rule of Butoh is, 'There is no self!'" In other words, art cannot be reduced to psychology—the psyche is in the world, not in an interior space understood in the Cartesian manner as separate from the external world. In fact, we understand who we are through what we do and what we make. *Poiesis* implies that we shape ourselves by shaping the world.

This is why, in the development of the field, the term "expressive therapy" has been replaced by "expressive *arts* therapy." It is not the person that touches us in the work but the expressive qualities that the work embodies. Rudolph Arnheim was one of the few psychologists to understand this. For him, the psychological element of the work of art consists not in the expression of the self but in the effect that the expressiveness of the work has upon the person.

Improvisation, then, cannot be understood as self-expression, doing whatever one feels like in the moment. Moreno, the founder of psychodrama, understood this very well in his description of spontaneity, action that is free (1987). Spontaneity, for him, is what characterizes an act that is an appropriate response to what is given, not mere action upon impulse. Moreno touches upon an important aspect of improvisation here. Unlike other theories of improvisation, spontaneity is not conceived of here as an absolutely unconstrained beginning, a God-like creation ex *nihilo*, but as a response to what is given, a response that meets the prior situation in a way that allows for maximum freedom within the framework that is provided to us. In expressive arts therapy, we speak of this as "expanding the range of play," the *Spielraum* or play-space in which the client finds themself. Usually someone will come into therapy with a sense that they have no options. They experience their range of play as constricted. By setting a frame for art-making in the session, we aim to give the person the experience of finding freedom within limits, an experience that can, homeopathically, enable them to see the possibilities in their own limited life-situation.

From this point of view, improvisation, although oriented toward the new, only accomplishes this goal by building upon the old. Improvisation in art-making responds to what has been given by taking it in unexpected directions. I have experienced this, for example, in participating in two improvisational music groups in Toronto, the Elements Choir and the Toronto Improvisers Orchestra. The Elements Choir is a purely vocal group led by a conductor, Christine Duncan. Christine uses a series of hand signals to indicate what kind of sound she would like to hear and who she would like to make it (e.g. who will solo, complement the soloist, sing in contrast to them, where silence or very loud sound will come, what pitch will be used, etc.). However, though there is the constraint of Christine's direction, the sounds themselves are not predictable and depend solely on the skill and sensitivity of the performer. As in all music-making, the key to excellence here is listening—the ability of the performer to hear what sound has occurred and to sense what could come next.

The Toronto Improvisers Orchestra (modeled on the London Improvisers Orchestra and using the same hand signals by a conductor) is a multi-instrumental group devoted to improvisational music. The musicians themselves are highly skilled performers, but the sounds they make often come from unusual or novel ways of using their instruments (in my own case, the voice). The orchestra has different conductors, and I have noticed a pronounced difference in the kind of music that is made as a consequence. In addition, there are times when we play without direction, in a manner reminiscent of the "free-jazz" movement of the 1960s. Although this can be fun, it never seems to me to be as successful artistically as the work we do when the conductor is leading.

Similarly, in the annual clown-show that I do with my partner Ellen Levine at the European Graduate School in Switzerland, although the show emerges out of improvisations that we and the other performers engage in (taking off from whatever has emerged in the school at that time), I usually take the role of director and shape the improvisations so that they have the maximum effect. At the same time, however, we allow for improvisational moments within the performance itself, playing within the framework so that it stays alive and does not become mere repetition. The hardest thing, in fact, is to take an improvised moment that has worked in rehearsal and "repeat" it in performance. Indeed, we have to do it as if it were happening for the first time. (This is also true for all theatre performers who play the same role over and over again.) Sometimes an unexpected element happens in the performance; someone falls down or a technical glitch occurs. Clowns call this a "gift from the gods," since it challenges us to be truly spontaneous in the moment without having prepared our response in advance.

Improvisation, then, although an activity which aims for maximum freedom, usually has a frame within which to operate. In addition, improvisation often has a director, someone who sets the frame and chooses the kind of expression that will occur. Moreover, improvisation, expecting the unexpected future, still responds to what has already been given in the past. Perhaps in this way improvisation is a model for life—we are never free from the past but neither are we condemned to repeat it. At every moment we can carry it forward into new and surprising directions.

Our necessarily belonging to a tradition that we are trying to overcome and the need we have for sensitive guidance in our attempt to find new ways can lead us into two difficulties inherent in our attempts at improvised art-making and improvised behavior in general. On the one hand, we can be stuck in our old patterns, repeating what once was new and is now merely a habit. And on the other hand, we can overly control and predict what will occur, trying to make it attain the result that we want. It was for this reason that John Cage, one of the great innovators in modern music, disdained the practice of improvisation.

Cage is sometimes thought of as a master of improvised music, but in fact he criticized improvisation as necessarily based on the composer's or performer's habits and memories. To make something truly new, Cage thought, it would be necessary to escape the subjectivity of the musician and base the music totally on chance. For this reason, Cage used random methods of composition in which his own inclinations would be put completely out of play. It is an open question, of course, whether this attempt at absolute serendipity was successful; among other things, Cage had to choose the particular random method that he was using. In addition, he came more and more to rely on one method, the *I Ching*, which has a very clear framework but is also subject to interpretation by anyone who employs it.

It was not until Cage was almost 70 that he deliberately took up improvisation as a compositional method, letting go, for the moment, of his own habits as a composer. In "How to Get Started" (1989), Cage developed an improvised lecture format, in which he used a series of ten cue cards, each with a single word that he had chosen on one side. Cage turned the cards over and, in a random manner, would pick one and then speak about the topic that the word indicated for three minutes. His three-minute lecture would be recorded and then played back while he was engaged in speaking for the next three minutes on another topic indicated by a different card. At the end, the audience heard ten lectures simultaneously occurring over ten different audio channels.

2012 was the centenary of John Cage's birth. To commemorate this, a number of events were held in different locations around the United States and other countries. In one of them, the lecture format for "How To Get Started" was offered for public participation. I first heard of this by chance, one might say, when a friend on Martha's Vineyard told me about his participation in a recorded performance using this format. At that point, I had the idea to give a lecture on improvisation at The European Graduate School and to use Cage's method as part of the event.

This seemed appropriate, since improvisation was not only a way of making art but also an essential element of expressive arts therapy. In the decentering phase of an expressive arts session, the client engages in improvised behavior that often leads to surprising and unexpected results. The aesthetic responsibility of the guide often involves a high degree of spontaneity on the part of the change agent themself, as they have to respond in the moment to whatever is happening to the client in the session.

Moreover, although the decentering has the characteristic of "free play" and is indeed designed to expand the imaginative possibilities in the client's life, the practice of "harvesting," in which the implications of the decentering for the client's situation are explored, has shown that there is almost always some relevance between what occurred in the free space of imaginative play and the literal reality that the client reported on in the beginning of the session. Thus decentering, far from being absolutely free, has the characteristics of improvisational action that we have outlined: a framework provided by a director, and behavior that, though spontaneous, nevertheless is always a response to what has already been given.

On this particular occasion, I began the lecture by discussing Cage and his influence on contemporary music. I then conducted a performance of Cage's classic work, *4'33"* (1952), with Paolo Knill at the piano. This is the well-known work in which Cage introduced the element of silence into contemporary music—the performer is absolutely still for four minutes and thirty-three seconds, the only sound being whatever happens by chance in the environment. Afterwards, students discussed their reaction to the performance, and I showed a video response by "an eminent music critic." In fact this was a Youtube clip, taken from the German film *Downfall*, which depicts the last days of Hitler. In the clip, someone had altered the words of Bruno Ganz, who played Hitler, so that he was speaking in English, fulminating, as only Hitler could, about how much he hated Cage's piece and what *Dreck* it was.

After elaborating on the significance of improvisation for the expressive arts, I then set up a performance of "How To Get Started," using ten index cards, with words I had chosen relevant to the field of expressive arts, laid face down on a table. I invited Ellen Levine to make an improvised visual art piece that would be an analogue to the lecture format. Consequently, Ellen chose ten containers, which she then numbered, and into which she placed ten different sorts of objects chosen at random from the art room. At every three-minute interval, she would overturn the container that had the same number as the index card whose word I was lecturing about, and add its contents to what she had already made. Since she was working on a flat table, we projected her process upon a large screen at the front of the room so that it could be seen by the audience.

We only had two audio channels, instead of the ten that Cage used. In order to facilitate the audience's experience, we removed the chairs and invited everyone to move around as they wished. This, in fact, became the occasion for the most spontaneous and unexpected part of the lecture. Since the audience was composed of European Graduate School faculty and students in the expressive arts, their way of moving around the room itself became an artistic performance. It was actually quite a beautiful choreography, as participants stood still, lay down, danced, did t'ai chi movements, etc. The combination of lecture, visual art-making and dance/movement "worked," and several students said that it was the best lecture they had attended at the school.

Nevertheless, on reflection I was disappointed with my own performance. Here the pitfalls of improvisation that Cage mentions can be seen. By choosing the words in advance, I had selected topics that I was familiar with. Consequently, for the most part I found myself saying things that I already knew and that probably the audience was familiar with as well. The only truly improvisatory moment came with the word "sex," which I had chosen just for fun. I remember for a moment not knowing what to say at all and then finding some interesting connections with the expressive arts. However, even in that case, I think I fell back in part upon some already formulated thoughts concerning the role of Eros in art-making.

This experience raises the issue of improvisation as a method of gaining knowledge, in other words, as a research method. How is it possible to avoid the habits and memories of the researcher in the quest for new knowledge? Too often research is a repetition of what the inquirer already knows. Especially in the case of "outcome" research, the researcher seeks to find the result that they anticipate—usually, in our field, trying to prove that their method of practicing expressive arts produces the desired outcome. This raises the question, how can we build upon what we know and still discover something new? Can we adopt an improvisational method for research in order to become spontaneous even in our attempt to understand the past?

In the process of supervising the doctoral dissertation of Sabine Silberberg, for example, I found a research project that was highly improvisatory in unexpected ways. Sabine had been working for over a decade as a counselor at the Doctor Peter Centre, a "harm-reduction" facility in Vancouver. The principle of harm-reduction is "to meet the client where they are at," i.e., not to impose a desired outcome on them but to respond to their situation in its own terms and to help them to find the best way to live with it. This means that counselors at the Centre do not try to help addicted clients "kick" their habits, but instead attempt to provide a supportive atmosphere in which clients can cope with the issues that addiction raises in ways that are not self-destructive.

In recent years, Sabine had become interested in photography and ultimately brought it into the Centre as a way of working with clients, who were instructed to photograph whatever they liked. The goal of her year-long dissertation research project was to see what impact photography could have upon clients within a harm-reduction context. Sabine chose to give clients cameras in order to encourage their capacity for taking charge of their lives. The first obstacle she faced was that sometimes clients would sell the cameras to sustain their drug habits, or lose them, or forget to bring them to sessions. She dealt with this partially by using cheap cameras whose loss could be tolerated and partially by using her own cameras or her computer in sessions with clients. At every step of the way, she had to improvise a response to the erratic behavior of her clients, using an "arts-analogue" method. In her words,

> *The term "arts-analogue" refers to an evolving process or dialogue between artist and subject or material. Each step calls for reflection, for a stepping back, and for a response to a newly changed shape, which in turn invites the next one. The process is characterized by uncertainty, by a searching and by emergence as responsive to aspects of the process.(Silberberg 2012, p.282)*

Not only did her clients discover new resources and possibilities for themselves through photography, but Sabine was also profoundly affected by the work they did and by the relationships that emerged as it was carried out As she says,

> *[what] the process has left me with is a profound longing for what the participants have brought to life within me: absorption in artistic processes and following my own longing for beauty. (p.282)*

To engage in improvisation in arts-based research, then, is to give up striving after a particular outcome and to be open to whatever arrives. Often this will be something surprising which calls for an unexpected response on the part of the researcher. In this way, the research process is similar to the process of art-making and also to the experience of the therapist or guide in the expressive arts. To enter the unknown in this way produces uncertainty, which can be tolerated only by the "longing for beauty" of which Sabine speaks. We cannot force beauty to come, we can only hold the hope that by not attempting to force her to arrive she may show up on her own. In other words, we need to cultivate an essentially aesthetic attitude, one that can transform the scholarly task of doing research into art-making, a process in which truth and beauty can overcome their traditional antagonism and find a home together at last.

11

KEEP YOUR SHIRT ON!

ART, THERAPY, AND THE SPACE IN-BETWEEN

A few years ago, I participated in a Community Art weekend at our training program in Toronto at The Create Institute. Each year we invite a different facilitator to lead the whole community in training students to use the arts to work with large groups. Rosario Sammartino, an Argentinian teacher from the Tamalpa Institute in California, led the workshop. The theme she chose was moving from isolation to community through crossing borders. On the Saturday of the workshop, we explored the meaning of isolation, individually and together. On Sunday, Rosario led us in a series of exercises designed to help us move from isolation into connection with others.

The method she used to do this was to break us up into small groups of six or seven. Each group would then engage in a series of movement improvisations, leading to a group performance in front of the whole community. We began by each of us taking turns physically positioning the other members of our small group. Then the group moved from those positions in a way that explored the possibilities for connection. In my group, we ultimately developed a performance, at the end of which I fell back into the arms of the other participants, all of whom were women.

When it came our group's turn to do the performance in front of the community, I had the impulse to take off my shirt, signifying the way in which people who move out of isolation into community often do so without defenses and are completely vulnerable, hoping to be received. In my mind, this seemed to be the typical experience of the refugee in coming to a new country.

After the performance, however, there was an uproar in the corridor. Rosario found the other members of my group in an agitated state, upset by what had happened during our performance. She suggested that they move into a more private space and invited me to join them. She then conducted a go-around in which each member of the group was given time to talk about their experience. Four of the five women said they experienced what I did as "inappropriate" and as an abuse of "power and privilege." In retrospect, I think that what may have particularly upset them was that by taking my shirt off and then falling into their arms, they touched my bare skin. This may very well have been experienced as a violation of the prohibition of touch in contemporary psychotherapy. I tried to listen in a non-defensive way, acknowledging their experience, while at the same time explaining my intention.

I thought it was a very good process, but the disturbance continued the next week in the first-year group to which these women belonged. Some of them talked about not being sure they would come back next year. I felt I needed to make an apology to the whole community to try to clear the air. When we all came back together a couple of weeks later for Studio Art presentations, I wrote out a statement apologizing for the hurt that they had felt by my action and stating what I was trying to do.

Not everyone in the community reacted in the same way as my group did. In fact, some of the other students said they found the performance compelling and relevant to the theme. They saw what I did as a rite of passage, which showed my vulnerability as an older person and, in so doing, touched on the experience of people in migration. Nevertheless, I had to take seriously the responses of the students in my group and others who were offended by what I did. It made me reflect not only upon my position in the community as the older male teacher and founder of the program but also the particular atmosphere in which psychotherapy training is conducted nowadays. I also began to think about the essential differences between an artistic performance and a therapeutic exploration. Indeed, several of the students in my own group said that if it had been a performance in a theatre, it would not have upset them. However, since it was in the context of a therapy training program, it had a different meaning for them.

What then is the difference between art and therapy? Is art-making essentially therapeutic? Or does it sometimes go beyond the bounds of therapy and take risks that would not be considered safe within a therapeutic context? Is there a limit on the use of the arts in therapy? Are these limits different from those in a purely artistic performance? These are some of the questions I was left with after this experience. They seem particularly relevant to me, since it took place within an arts therapy training program. For that reason alone, we have to look closely at the nature and limits of the artistic experience.

Much of contemporary art, especially in performance, proceeds on the basis that there are no limits established beforehand that tell us what we can and cannot do. As long as no one is physically hurt in the performance, anything is possible. I recall teaching a clown workshop in our training program in which one of the students developed a kind of sadistic or murderous clown persona. It was quite effective as a performance, but when she went into the audience and actually started strangling somebody, we had to stop her. In general, however, contemporary art recognizes few bounds. In fact, its efficacy depends on its willingness to go beyond the limits of work previously done. I think for example of the early work of Marina Abramovic, one of whose public performances involved living naked in a cage lined with knives for a month.

The field of therapy, on the other hand, has more and more emphasized the importance of safety for the client in the building of a holding relationship in which many of the hurts of earlier life can be explored and overcome. In our own training program at The Create Institute, we have always taken the position that safety is essential, but only in so far as it creates a platform for taking risks. When safety becomes regarded as the only important thing in the whole of the therapeutic experience, the question arises whether growth is possible. Do we have to go outside of our comfort zone in order to take a step forward in our development?

Our approach to the therapy in expressive arts has stemmed from a confidence in *poiesis*, the belief that the most therapeutic thing we can do is help another person "step forth with courage" and begin to actualize possibilities which have been unrealized by her own limitations. In the process of decentering, as we have said, the role of the therapist is to help clients find their own aesthetic response, to facilitate a process in which something happens which touches them and provides the possibility of transformation. I wonder whether this is possible if there are too many limitations placed on exploration beforehand.

Nevertheless, it is clear that although art and therapy may touch each other and even overlap in certain areas, there are ways in which their goals and their methods are quite different. The artist wants to bring forth in beauty, to facilitate the coming to be of something that did not exist before. In therapy, on the other hand, the goal is to help the client to become who they are by actualizing the resources which have been lying dormant within them.

Here the question of limits comes up very clearly. By creating a free atmosphere, do we run the risk of encouraging the client to go beyond their own limits too much? Do we have to take safety into account in arts therapy in a way in which we do not in a purely artistic enterprise? Are the arts inherently therapeutic or is it only within the therapeutic relationship they can serve this purpose? How can we maintain a creative atmosphere in the therapeutic work while still respecting the boundaries of the client?

And of course, the question arises, if we do go too far and hurt a client emotionally, can there be repair, and can the boundary violation actually become an opportunity for growth? Although I'm not sure everyone felt that the issue was resolved, my apology to the community did touch several people. I am reminded of the book by Ernest Wolff, *Treating the Self* (1998), written from a self-psychological perspective in which empathic attunement on the part of the therapist is crucial for development. At the same time, the author states that sometimes working through a therapist's empathic break is the most curative factor in the relationship.

Is the issue that my action brought up resolved? I'm sure there are those who still are troubled by it, as well as others who have found their way through. In the small group discussion after the performance, I suggested that we treat what happened as a learning opportunity, in the same way as anything else that happens in therapy training. Perhaps some of the students have been led to reflect on the relationship between art and therapy and come to see it in a new way. As for me, I have a deeper appreciation not only of what is proper to my place in the community but also of the limits of artistic exploration within a therapeutic context.

I don't think the question of the relationship between art and therapy can ever be resolved, and I'm not sure it should be. Perhaps the space of the in-between is where we live. Perhaps it is the transitional or liminal space in which all creative growth is possible. If we can find our way in this in-between and bring the full resources of both the arts and therapy to bear, we may be able to open the door to places in which both we and our clients have never been. We may still make mistakes in crossing boundaries, but we will never fail for lack of courage or for lack of belief in the transformative power of the arts. I believe this space is our sacred ground. We should honor it as our own special place of transformation.

12

WHO AM I?
WHAT AM I?

THE *POIESIS* OF IDENTITY

The predominance of "identity politics" in our culture leads me to wonder about the notion of identity. Are we our identity or identities? What is an identity? Do identities matter? I ask these questions at a time when identity politics is denounced by the right, and when at the same time "identity" is used as an instrument of critique by the anti-oppression movement on the left. Without taking sides (and perhaps the idea of "sides" itself relies on the notion of identity), I'd like to examine "identity" in reference to therapy, art and, ultimately, life.

I remember a Danish psychiatrist walking around in a community art session at the Spring Symposium of Expressive Arts Therapy in Europe many years ago, repeating over and over, "Who am I? What am I?" These are, in my opinion, good questions for psychiatrists to ask. He could have answered them by naming his profession, but instead, by repeating his questions over and over, he communicated the urgency with which he questioned his own identity and, perhaps, the categories into which his patients had been placed.

Certainly, there is a tendency in psychiatry and psychotherapy to put people into diagnostic categories. The widespread use of the *DSM* (*Diagnostic and Statistical Manual of Mental Disorders*, 2013), and the authority that it claims, attests to the tendency to identify people with the different kinds of mental ailments from which they suffer. If nothing else, these categorical diagnoses are essential for insurance purposes. Many therapists, in fact, hold the categories lightly in practice. I know several who ask their clients to choose the ones that they themselves think fit. Nevertheless, the commonly accepted practice in which therapists identify the people with whom they work in terms of their diagnoses, places their work into a perspective in which any questions about the basis of human existence become irrelevant.

Philosophy in the West, however, begins with the questioning of what is commonly accepted. Socrates' distinction between "opinion," that which is held to be true without examination, and "knowledge," that which can show the basis on which it stands, implies that common beliefs, no matter how firmly they are held, cannot be accepted without question. The distinction between seeming and being, appearance and reality, is fundamental to philosophical thinking. This distinction holds for our own existence as well.

When it comes to the question of personal identity, then, we have to distinguish who we seem to be from who we are. My identity may change; I may become older, take up new professional roles, even change my gender identification, but I consider myself to still be the same person, even if I seem different to others.

Indeed, my "identity" may be understood as consisting in part of what I am identified as by others, in part as what I take myself to be, whereas we usually think of the "self" as something substantial beneath my identifications. From this perspective, I have to examine who I am and go beneath my identity to find my "self." Thus, the traditional philosophical distinction between being and seeming would seem to solve the problem of personal identity. However, the question then arises, if we are not really our identities, what are we? What is this "self?"

Psychotherapy is often understood as a quest for self, replacing religion and philosophy as the contemporary form of self-discovery. Often people enter therapy as the result of some crisis, which has shattered their sense of who they are, their "identity." There is a "breakdown" of some sort; that which I rely on can no longer be taken for granted. I then have to give up what I had previously regarded as the foundation of my existence; I am thrown into chaos and confusion, a state full of anguish from which I try vainly to escape.

The role of the therapist, it seems to me, is not to eliminate this confusion by giving me a new self-definition, since that would only replace one identity with another, but to help me stay in the chaos, no matter how painful, and to find my own way through. One view of psychotherapy, then, is that it is based on a radical questioning of identity and a search for authentic self-hood. However, we could also say that the authentic self is something we make, rather than something we find within us.

In this way, the self can be considered as the result of an act of *poiesis*, similar to the creation of a work of art. Can an aesthetic perspective help us understand this search for self? First of all, as I've indicated throughout this book, it is essential not to reduce art-making to self-expression. The work of art comes from me, but it is not me. In the same way, children come from their parents and may have some of their characteristics, but they cannot be identified with those who bring them into being. As Shaun McNiff says, "I imagine artistic expressions as children, and like children they are related to but separate from their makers" (McNiff 2004, p.90). Rather, children have their own separate existence and, in fact, may seek to find themselves by casting off their parental identifications and influences. Indeed, psychotherapy can often be a means of discovering these and casting them off.

Similarly, artists may experience the "anxiety of influence" (Bloom 1997), the sense that their work needs to transcend the influences which past art-works have upon them in order to create something that is authentically theirs. In this sense, the identity of the artist as well needs to be created rather than accepted as given.

This letting-go of the past may in part be a consequence of living in a modern society in which change is seen as a positive value, and tradition as a drag upon progress. However, I wonder if "traditional" cultures are as conservative as we think they are. It is true that such cultures justify everything in terms of the past, but at the same time, their practices and ideals are actually always undergoing a process of modification. This is particularly true for pre-literate societies. Since there is no written text to copy, their members must rely on the memory of the group; but, as we know, memory is unreliable and often the product of the imagination. Traditional cultures may be more innovative than we think.

If there is nothing fixed that we can return to, does that mean that we are free to make of ourselves whatever we choose? Is our freedom radical in this sense? This would seem to be the existential view of the self. But is the absoluteness of our freedom not limited by the situation in which we find ourselves? We are always in a world with others, a world that we have not created but into which, in Heidegger's word, we are "thrown" (1962, p.174). We always have to take our situation into account. Here I am in this time and at this place, with the identity given to me by my biology and the society I am born into. I have to work with these. Otherwise any identity that I imagine would be as valid as any other, and all of them would be mere fantasies.

At this point in history, for example, being a man means not only that I am biologically male, but that I can decide what kind of man I shall be. Misogynist or feminist? I am free to go in either direction, or indeed to reject these alternatives and create a new version of masculinity. But whatever I choose, I will always be the one-who-was-born-male at a certain period of history when the possibilities are different than they have been in the past. Similarly, to be white does not necessarily mean that I have to accept the culture of white supremacy in which I have been raised, although I may have internalized it in ways that are not immediately apparent to me and that I need to become aware of. Thus, all the categories by which we can be identified need to be interpreted in terms of the situation in which we find ourselves and the choices we have made. Our possibilities are limited by the world into which we are born and by the decisions we have made in the past.

Is this not the same for the artist? God is said to create *ex nihilo*—since nothing exists before His creation, He is not limited by what has been given to Him. But artists find themselves in the world at a particular time and place. Even works of fantasy take off from the world in which their makers live and are always experienced by those who live in that world. The styles of work that are offered to artists historically and the media in which they work also have to be taken into account in order to understand what they make, even if their work is a radical rejection of what is given in favor of the new. The artist is not a god creating something out of nothing, as the Romantic tradition would have it, but a human being transforming what they have been given so as to bring something new into being.

This is also true for therapy. Clients may wish to disavow the past and make of themselves something radically different from what they have been, something that will replace their suffering with happiness, but this cannot be done by rejecting what has happened to them or what they have themselves done. Rather, we often speak of "working through," coming to understand the past and transforming rather than eliminating it.

We could even say that our clients are, ideally, artists of themselves. Therapy, in this sense, is a creative process. The role of the therapist is to be, as Socrates said about the philosopher who helps another to bring a new idea into being, a "midwife" to the client's act of self-creation. Creativity in therapy is the act of transforming what we have been given. This is what we mean by *poiesis*, bringing something new into being by working on what already exists.

In the arts therapies, the imagination of clients is invited to set to work to find alternatives to the life they have lived. By shaping materials into a work, clients can also find a capacity in themselves that could also be used in their life-situations outside of the therapy session. The work may even give them a message about how this can be done and what they need to do to bring it about.

Thus, therapy is not only about remembering the past. In fact, an exclusive focus on the past may prevent the person from imagining alternatives for the future. The past is remembered in order to imagine it differently. We are always reworking what has been, even when we think we are repeating it. We need to "decenter," to move away from an exclusive focus on what happened to us in order to imagine new alternatives. This move into the alternative world of the imagination opens up new possibilities for our existence. Who we can be takes priority over who we have been. There will always be a tension between who we have been and who we can become, although it may be a productive, not destructive, tension.

This raises the question, how do we know what imaginative possibilities are real and not mere fantasy? One way would be to distinguish mere fantasy from that power of imagination that affects us and gives us a new sense of ourselves. The image must touch or move us for it to have an effect upon us. Whether we call this a "felt sense" or an "aesthetic response," the imagination must impact our sense of self for what it reveals to be meaningful to us. The image or the art-work, then, is not the mirror of an already existing self. Rather, it gives us the sense of a possible future self. To take it otherwise would be to project our contemporary understanding of ourselves into the past.

We can say that who we are is our identity, but it is also the possibility of re-forming that identity. In that sense, we can view the self as the created-creating aspect of the person. It is what we have made in response to what we have been given, including what we have been given by our own acts of making. But it is also our power to create ourselves in the future, to take our "givenness" and shape it differently than it has been.

Psychotherapy can be seen as a discipline of self-creation or what we call *autopoiesis* (or perhaps *sympoiesis*, since the self is formed in the encounter between therapist and client). No wonder that the question of who I am cannot ever be finally answered. I "am" my identity (or identities), but I also go beyond them through my *poietic* capacity. Identity can never be set in stone, not even in a gravestone, for we also have the responsibility to shape those who have preceded us in accordance with our own situation and the imaginative possibilities that are revealed to us.

What then of my relationship to others? Is my self-creation an autonomous act, one in which I form myself without taking others into account? Not at all. I am influenced by others at every moment of my existence, from my birth and early life to my adulthood and beyond, perhaps even to my death. Influence, though, however strong, does not mean determination. I am responsible for what comes to me from others, whether it is a matter of accepting, rejecting or imagining it in a radically new way. At the same time, since the influence may be coercive, I may need different others to help me overcome it.

Heidegger's idea of authenticity seems to view the authentic self as formed by a radical act of self-creation. For him this means that I find myself only by withdrawing from others, from the common herd, the "they" (*das Man*) (1962, p.167). In his critique of this view, Emmanuel Levinas says that I come to exist only through the call which others make to me. I am called into existence by them, especially by their calls for help. Thus, for him, authentic existence is an ethical act. My relation to others precedes my relation to myself (Levinas 1991).

However, not every call from another is a plea for help. It is understandable why Levinas framed it this way, writing as a Jew in the shadow of the Holocaust and the suffering of its victims. Yet, is not my first relationship properly one of love that comes to me from the other? It is only when the mothering figure treats the child primarily as an answer to her own needs that this relationship becomes a call for help for herself and not a call of love.

As Winnicott reminds us, this can result in a deformation of the self of the child, as she shapes herself to please her care-giver. Yet even in this situation, children shape their own response—they can be good girls or boys, only doing what mother wants, even to the extent of identifying with her needs, or bad girls or boys, always in opposition.

We are affected by others, but we are responsible for the ways we shape ourselves in relation to them. In a sense, we carry the other within us, but we are not this other, even when we identify with them. The task of therapy then is to find the ability to shape ourselves beyond our identifications.

Winnicott calls our authentic being the "true self." This sounds like something substantial that underlies our identity. But is not the true self the capacity for self-formation, in other words, the creative self? If the self is something we make rather than find, would not the "truth" of the self be our ability to make ourselves, that is, our poietic self? *Poiesis*, then, can be considered as essential to selfhood. There is nothing persisting about the self except its capacity to form itself in response to others.

This perspective has political implications as well as psychological ones. Not only individuals have what we might call a "poietic responsibility," communities also have this capacity. Oppressed groups have typically been denied the capacity to form themselves in accordance with their own needs. For social change activists, in that case, political action to remedy the suffering that this oppression entails should be addressed to fostering self-organization, helping groups to find themselves, not those identities that have been imposed on them by others, or by themselves through identification with the needs of others, but rather those which increase their capacity to shape themselves according to their own possibilities. The philosopher Cornelius Castoriadis speaks of the "imaginary institution of society"

(1998). Communities as well as individuals have the capacity for forming themselves through creative imagination. Identities imposed by others, such as those given by racism or misogyny, may be their starting-place, but these ascribed identities can never define them.

Can politics based on identity serve as a basis for liberation? Perhaps, but only if this self-formation takes into account the needs of others. To act only on the basis of one's identity can limit the creative potential of a group and put it into the position of having to affirm its difference from others, a difference which then separates the group from these others.

It is understandable why identity has become a political watchword. An oppressed group, black people in America for example and elsewhere, may have been identified negatively by those in power. This identification, in turn, is then taken to be a justification for their oppression. If the group can turn this ascribed identity into a source of self-affirmation, for example by affirming that "black lives matter," it can regain a measure of agency. However, the danger is that it may do so only at the cost of confining itself within the identity that it has been made to inhabit. True liberation, rather, may consist in re-working this ascribed identity and engaging in an act of self-formation, which opens new possibilities for both one's own community and for others outside of it.

An example of this creative re-shaping can be seen in the work of Judith Butler. In her book, *Parting Ways: Jewishness and the Critique of Zionism* (2014), Butler, who is herself Jewish, sees Zionism as a failed attempt at instituting a mythical identity based on a nationalist conception of Judaism. In her view, it operates only by turning the Palestinians into others whose existence must be denied in order for me to be myself.

Although Butler rejects Zionism's exclusivity, she does so by a re-imagining of the ethico-political dimension of Jewish identity itself. For her, the demands for justice and equality by means of which she critiques the Zionist project, can themselves be found within the Jewish tradition. At the same time, she sees these claims as transcending their origins. Justice and equality must be achieved for all, Jew and non-Jew alike. Thus, her critique of Jewish nationalism is ultimately based on the universalism within the Jewish tradition itself.

This universalism is not the property of a particular group. Rather it is the consequence of the general human characteristic of exile and wandering. The diasporic condition to which Jews have been subjected since the destruction of the Temple could be seen as something to be overcome through the establishment of a "homeland." But it could also enable us to see that human existence cannot be identified with a specific national identity, or with a territory and borders that exclude others. Thus, Butler paradoxically forms her identity as a Jew through a critique of the legitimacy of a Jewish homeland, and this critique is based on Judaism itself.

Identity, conceived in this way, becomes a positive factor in political self-formation. If the human condition is one of dispersal and dispossession, then I am essentially open to others, since they too share these characteristics (Butler 2014). I do not need to exclude the other in order to assert my own existence. Rather, openness to alterity is how I come to be. We are all in this together. A poietic conception of human existence is based on what we have in common, our non-identical selfhood.

From this perspective, we can even say that *poiesis* is inherently democratic, though not in the sense of representative democracy, in which special interest groups claim to speak for all. Rather, our capacity for *poiesis* gives the possibility of forming the "democracy-to-come" of which Jacques Derrida speaks (2005), the imaginative possibility of self-formation which belongs to all of us. Rather than thinking in terms of identity as an exclusive act of self-creation, it might be better to refer to Hardt and Negri's concept of the "multitude," the heterogenous community of those who transcend their ascribed social identifications by the recognition of their poietic capacity and their need to act in common in order to achieve freedom for themselves and for others as well (2004).

We cannot be identified with one another, but we can recognize the potential of our commonality and act to bring it into existence without giving up who we have been. For Hardt and Negri, this radical democracy of the common is now an historical possibility, as the productive process has been generalized from dependence on the labor of a particular group, the industrial working class in early capitalism, to the more universal immaterial labor of today, based on culture and communication. All of us are now producers in our work and in our lives, that is, all of us generate value in our social world. This historical development makes it possible for us to go beyond identification with a particular social group and to see ourselves as belonging to the common without having to efface ourselves in a mass without distinctions. To understand ourselves as belonging to the multitude opens the possibility of a more creative dimension of human being than seeing ourselves only as members of a particular group.

The virtue of a politics based on identity is to recognize the ways in which we have been identified and have identified ourselves. However, the danger is that we may reify this identity and lose our capacity for self-transformation. In doing so, we also lose the possibility of a liberatory relation to others based on our fundamental commonality (Haider, 2018).

We are our identities in the mode of having been them. To transcend identity can then mean to affirm a possible future beyond our own boundaries and to join in a common project without losing our sense of selfhood. In fact, we are always transcending identity, whether we realize it or not. The other may attempt to trap us in the definitions they give to us, but even when we accept these, we only can do so by admitting that otherness into ourselves. In that sense, we are never alone, we are always who we are in relation to others. Moreover, we cannot completely coincide with how we have been identified, since we are also what we are becoming. We are what we can be, not only what we have been. And what we can be, as we have maintained throughout this book, is the result of an act of *poiesis*.

If *poiesis* is the basis of human existence, then perhaps it is the special task of the poets to show us what we can be. Judith Butler ends her political critique with a chapter on the Palestinian poet Mahmoud Darwish. In "Edward Said: A Contrapuntal Reading," his elegy on the death of Edward Said, the Palestinian intellectual and social critic who developed a critique of "Orientalism," Darwish writes an imaginary poetic dialogue between Said and himself (2007). It is "contrapuntal" because the poem is both an address by Said to Darwish and a response by Darwish to Said. Butler quotes Said, "If I die before you/ my will is the impossible" and also, "'the aesthetic is to reach Poise.'" "Poise" is, Butler says, "the translation of mulaa'im (agreement, gathering)" (Butler 2014, p.217). As I understand it, Said's address means that his will is to have a gathering of what has been scattered and to come to an agreement with those with whom we disagree, a clear reference to the diasporic condition of the Palestinians and their "disagreement" with the Israelis. This seems "impossible" at this point of history, yet it is what Said "wills."

To will the impossible is, perhaps, a task for the poet, an aesthetic task whose goal is "to reach Poise" (Butler 2014, p.217). How can the aesthetic do that? Not by describing "what the camera can say of your wounds," but by inventing "a hope for speech…And sing, for the aesthetic is freedom" (p.220). The poet's song reaches freedom, but only by his address to the other, in this case, to Darwish and through him to the reader as well. The contrapuntal form of the poem indicates that the poet is not a sovereign subject who can dictate the future (Shelley's unacknowledged legislator of mankind, 2009, p.46), but rather a partner in a dialogue which depends on the participation of both interlocuters. Similarly, Hardt and Negri speak of their work as a series of "calls and responses… not questions and answers, as if the responses could put the calls to rest." Rather, "calls and responses should speak back and forth in an open dialogue" between self and other (Hardt and Negri 2004, p.xxi).

In order to have an open dialogue, both participants must speak from a condition of equality, and, in order for the dialogue to be effective, that is, for it to affect both participants, each one must be open to the other. In Darwish's poem, he asks Said, "What about identity?", and the response comes, "It's a self-defense… / Identity is the child of birth, but / at the end, it's self-invention, and not / an inheritance of the past. I am multiple" (Butler 2014, p.218). For dialogue to be possible, I must include the other within myself. This opening to alterity means that I cannot be captured within a single identity; my identity always includes otherness. Compare Whitman's lines, "Do I contradict myself? Very well then I contradict myself. I am large, I contain multitudes." (2015, p.84).

Said's words obviously refer to the Palestinians and the Israelis, but they could also be taken to refer to each of us. We are all, in a way, exiles from ourselves, scattered among the nations. As Said says, "The outside world is exile / exile is the world inside." And then the question comes, "And what are you between the two?"(Butler 2014, p.218).This question is addressed not only to Darwish, Said's dialogue partner, but to each of us. Butler wonders parenthetically "(…whether the contrapuntal is the poetic form for the impossible task, carrying on in a form of self-splitting)" (p.219).

In Butler's text, Said's voice says, "Invent a hope for speech" and "… sing, for the aesthetic is freedom" (p.220). Sing or scream? The text is ambiguous. Perhaps this is the impossible task of poetry, to scream one's wounds into song. Darwish ends his poems with these lines, "Farewell, / Farewell poetry of pain" (p.223). Clearly, he is not telling us to forget our pain, but to turn it into song. As Butler says, "… in this contrapuntal ode, the scream is effectively transmuted to song" (p.223). It is only through the address to the other and the promise of a response, that this impossible task can be accomplished.

One could then understand Butler's book as an address to the reader, a plea to the reader to undertake the impossible task of becoming open to the other. This would mean, I think, to hear the screams of the dispossessed, not only the Palestinians but all those who are refugees, and also to recognize ourselves in them, to understand that even our own seemingly secure and fixed identities are the defenses, the walls, we erect against admitting the other within the territory of the self. This defense can only be maintained through violence, the denial of the right to exist not only of the other but, ultimately, of the self as well.

Is it only through the aesthetic, through art-making, that we can dismantle defenses and open to our otherness? Could the impossible task of the aesthetic be carried into life as well? Can there be a politics based on *poiesis*? This is a question which I address to the reader and, implicitly, to myself as well. Only the dialogue which it may open up can be an adequate response. As Butler says in her concluding remarks, "Exile is the name of separation, but alliance is found precisely there, not yet in a place that was and is and in the impossible place of the not yet, happening now" (p.224). This impossible place is the place of my hope for these words.

BETHLEHEM AFGHANISTAN

I am not a Christian
But the image of Christ on the cross
Comes to me this Christmas Day
As I read of Joao Silva
His legs blown off photographing
The war in Afghanistan

He had been in Soweto and Iraq
Wherever men and women died
In war and revolution
He had been there to witness
To tell of the suffering of others
Of the plague that was spread
From pride

Joao Silva loved life so much
He was drawn to the places
Where it made no sense
Where only murder
Held meaning

A man who made others laugh
Not solemn or holy
But single-purposed
Repeating over and over
Look at this
Look at this
Look at this

I remember Austin Clarke
Suddenly standing up in the audience
While Cecil Taylor sounded the depths
Of musical chaos
Declaiming loudly in his basso profundo
This must stop!
This must stop!

Now Joao Silva lies in Walter Reed Hospital
He will spend two years
Learning to walk without legs
He will not return to Afghanistan

I wonder when I will stand and say
Look at this
This must stop!
And I wonder when you will listen
When we will listen
To the good news
He is born
He is born again to testify
To tell us of our fate
Born in a manger in Basra
Wounded in Bagram
Resurrected in the picture
In the poem

Look at this
This must stop!
Love is life
Love not death
Is life
Love I say
Not death
Is life

PART V

LAST WORDS: WHEN ALL IS SAID AND DONE

13

THE ART OF TRAUMA

POIESIS AND HUMAN EXISTENCE

How is it possible to speak about trauma? Victims of trauma, those who have suffered a wound that marks them forever, are themselves often speechless, unable to articulate a narrative that would make meaning out of what has happened to them. And yet they must speak, must utter words that have significance or remain forever in the dumb condition in which they have been left.

When I was asked to give a lecture on trauma at Wilfred Laurier University as the keynote address for the Conference, "Trauma: Body, Mind, and Spirit," I felt myself incapable of speaking, of giving the impression of someone who is in command of his thought, who has mastered his subject and who can dispose of it for the comprehension and benefit of others. I thought of "trauma specialists," those who have joined the legion of helpers whose professional expertise separates them from the subject of trauma, someone who is helpless and uncomprehending. If anything, I felt myself more akin to the vulnerable one than to the "master and commander" of trauma.

But I had agreed to speak. Why? I had written a book called, *Trauma, Tragedy, Therapy: The Arts and Human Existence* (2009). So I had already spoken, already presented myself as one who knows. But what did I know? Now that I was facing the injunction of telling, I was myself dumb. What presumption! To pretend to understand human suffering, the mystery of which has remained concealed despite the efforts of millennia of philosophers and theologians. Why do we suffer? Why must we suffer? We who can no longer find an explanation in the will of God or in the consequences of previous incarnations know nothing that would help us answer these questions. And yet to proclaim our ignorance may itself be a form of pride. In the company of Socrates and in contradistinction to those who claim expertise, I know that I do not know. My ignorance is my only power.

Yet we who proclaim our ignorance of trauma must surely have some awareness of the subject, since, after all, we are human. And to be human is to know we must die and to suffer the death of others who are dear to us. Our vulnerability is evident in spite of all our efforts to hide it. Ernest Becker in *The Denial of Death* goes so far as to say that our very culture is characterized throughout by the attempt to deny the fact of our mortality (1997). We are obsessed with health and the prolongation of life, exercising madly and gobbling vitamins and supplements in a vain attempt to ward off illness, aging and death, the realization of the necessity of which caused Prince Shakyamuni to leave the confines of his palace's protection and go, figuratively, naked into the world to find the meaning of suffering. His enlightenment came only when he realized, with a shock of recognition, that existence itself is the cause of suffering. To be is to suffer: this, the Buddhists tell us, is the ultimate truth. We are essentially vulnerable.

I myself, without having suffered the trauma of rape or the aftershock of battle, was particularly aware of my own vulnerability, by virtue of my experience of aging and loss of capacities, by the consequences of a bicycle accident that had happened two years ago from which I was still recovering, and by the haunting awareness which I have had since childhood of the genocide that had been committed on my own people, an awareness that gradually extended to all the genocides that have accompanied the "march of civilization," i.e., history.

It seems to me that we all have what we might call a "pre-reflective" awareness of trauma and of the vulnerability that makes woundedness possible. Even without having directly experienced catastrophe, we know what trauma is from the very fact of being conscious and alive, aware of our own mortality. When we are able to face this experience directly, we can acknowledge our essential vulnerability rather than trying desperately to escape from it. Strangely enough, from a Buddhist perspective, this knowledge, rather than causing suffering, can bring us joy, the joyful acceptance of what is, the affirmation of existence. And this acceptance can lead us to praise, to sing hosannas to life. As Rilke tells us in his *Sonnets to Orpheus*, "Only in the realm of praising should lament walk…" (1985, p.33, first published 1925).

Orpheus, in this vision, can sing of lost Eurydice only by having seen her beauty when she was alive. His lament is only made possible by his ability to praise. Rilke himself aspires to this condition, but, he tells us, only "A god can do it… will you tell me how / a man can enter through the lyre's strings? / Our mind is split." (1985, p.23). We are split between life and death, between our fervent desire to go on existing and our knowledge that everything must cease. We must, Rilke writes to those who are young, "…learn / to forget that passionate music. It will end. / True singing is a different breath, about / nothing. A gust inside the god. A wind." (1985, p.33).

Can we sing about nothing? Can *poiesis* be a hymn to transience? Rilke's entire poetic work can be seen as an attempt to accept what is passing. As he writes, "Be ahead of all parting, as though it already were / behind you, like the winter that has just gone by" (1985, p.245). The *Sonnets to Orpheus* themselves were inspired by the death of a young dancer, Vera Knoop, whose beauty was cut short by her early death. Rilke would, like Orpheus, bring the realms of life and death together, but, as he tells us, "Our mind is split" (1985, p.23). We are unable to comprehend their unity. All we can do is to praise existence while mourning its passing.

This acceptance of transience stands in opposition to the Western philosophical tradition, in which, beginning with Plato, becoming is seen as the enemy of knowledge and true being. The philosopher disdains the world of coming-into-being and passing-away in favour of the unchanging essence of what is true. Philosophy, in Socrates' words, is a way of "practising death," but only in the sense in which to die is for the soul, separated from the decaying body, to live forevermore (Plato 1966, p.133). Plato's rejection of *poiesis* as a path to truth is based on his rejection of the existing world, full of chaos and contradiction and constantly in flux. For him, the *polis*, the political life in which humans are meant to live together, is threatened by the poets, who depict humanity in all its flaws and divisions, thereby disrupting the order on which social life depends. Therefore, Plato tells us, they must be exiled from the just city.

It is only with Nietzsche that this tradition begins to be overcome. And it is from his understanding of *poiesis* in Greek tragedy that

Nietzsche learns to see the underlying meaning of existence in the celebration of the temporal. Through his vision of the Dionysian chorus that underlies and sustains the beauty of the Apollonian text, Nietzsche was able to divine the chaotic energy behind the forms of articulate language. The text of *The Birth of Tragedy* (originally entitled, *The Birth of Tragedy out of the Spirit of Music*) is itself characterized by its lyrical energy. As Nietzsche wrote in a later "Attempt at a Self-Criticism," rather than writing, this "new soul" "… should have sung" (1967, p.20).

Is *poiesis*, then, an adequate response to trauma? What is it about the arts that enables them to catch the bird of suffering on its wing? There are, in fact, many ways in which artistic creation resembles the traumatic condition. To be in a creative state, we have to give up the security that comes when we feel ourselves to be capable of carrying out a plan. Artistic creation may begin with an emotion, an imaginative vision, or an idea, yet once the work begins, the creator can only follow it, at the risk of running aground. The artist must suffer what comes and surrender the illusion of mastery that we seek in vain in our everyday life. As James Hillman never tired of saying, "Stick to the image" (1977, p.68). Let it lead you to the work that is emerging and do not try to bend it to your will. Or as my Butoh teacher would tell us before beginning a movement improvisation, "Give up that good idea!" I always felt she was speaking to me personally, but in fact it was a universal injunction to those who engage in improvisational theatre—or in life.

The artist neither knows nor is in control of the emerging work. In her ignorance and lack of mastery, the artist has something in common with the victim of trauma. Of course, the radical difference is that the artist enters into this condition voluntarily and can also exit from it, though sometimes with great effort, by her deliberate action. As opposed to the horror of trauma, artistic work brings the joy of creation, even if there is abjection when it is not "working."

What is it that makes art possible? I see the possibility of the work of art as rooted in an awareness of the vulnerability that characterizes our condition. Only by voluntarily embracing this vulnerability can something new emerge. Thus, it is possible to understand authentic existence not only in the awareness of death, as Heidegger writes in *Being and Time* (1962), but also in our sense of life as continuously emerging, constantly changing and bringing forth something new. Hannah Arendt calls this sense "natality," in contradistinction to Heidegger's emphasis on "mortality" (1962, p.247). It is just as essential to our existence to be able to create as to be aware that we will die.

Heidegger uses the everyday German word for existence, *Dasein* (etymologically, "to be there,") as the term for human existence. Paradoxically, for him, *Dasein* is authentically itself only in the comprehension of the possibility of its not being there, i.e., in its own non-existence. For Rilke, on the other hand, *Gesang ist Dasein*, song is existence (1985, p.23). We truly exist only when we create. In his essay, "The Origin of the Work of Art," Heidegger himself comes close to this point of view (1975).

This understanding of *poiesis* is radically different from the traditional one, in which an act of artistic creation is understood to be carried out with will and knowledge. The artist has an idea (or follows a pre-existing form) and then decides to put it into action, as the divine Creator does. God himself (and I use the masculine pronoun advisedly, since this conception of the divine has been based on the traditional conception of masculinity) is understood as omniscient and omnipotent. He creates according to His intention and has no barrier to His act. The human act of creation is seen in the Western philosophical tradition from a similar perspective: we create what we consciously intend to make. What we make, then, is a copy of what is already there, whether it be an idea of our own or a model of what exists outside us.

The consequence of this view is to see art as *mimesis*, imitation. This is one of the objections that Plato makes against the poets. For him, they are only imitators of what exists, and an imitation has a lesser mode of existence than the original. Moreover, the imitation may misrepresent the original, it may stray far from the truth. Art, then, insofar as it depicts the phenomenal world of coming-into-being and passing-away, is a lie, and the artist a liar. For Plato, only the eternal forms possess true existence, and these can never be represented adequately in a changing world.

What has happened to change this view of *poiesis*? Certainly, it is partially a consequence of the changing world view in the West in recent centuries. As we have encountered different cultures through exploration, colonialization and commerce, and as our own world has gone through a process of constant change and upheaval, we no longer have the confidence that our culture can serve as the unchanging model to which all civilization should aspire. Eternity does not seem quite so eternal; change and innovation are the constant state. Above all, the flow of capital demands this, as does the continuity of power held by those who control the market.

Furthermore, and perhaps as a consequence of what is described above, the nature of *poiesis* has also come into question in artistic practice itself. Art can no longer be understood as *mimesis*, since there is no eternal model to copy. Rather, the title of Pirandello's play, *Tonight We Improvise* (1960, first published 1930), can serve as the motto for artistic creation in our time. We copy at our peril. Therefore, we must continually improvise and find new forms, even to the point at which our own development is valued only if we keep changing. "Change or die" has become a universal credo. Ezra Pound's maxim, "Make it new!" now serves as the model for our creative acts.

Of course, the necessity of change may be denied. We experience a great loss in our inability to rely on tradition, a loss which motivates many to try to hold onto a vision of an unchanging past at any cost. Religious fundamentalism is one form of this effort, as is the political populism of our time. "Make America great again," implies an original greatness which we must restore or else lose our right to exist.

In the arts, there are also movements which attempt to go back to classical models, in some cases with great success. But even such successful efforts cannot serve as taken-for-granted standards that must be maintained in future work. They are experienced as returns, and thus not as adequate for the experience of a present which faces an unknown future.

When there are no models, we must improvise. We operate (make a "work," English for the Latin *opera*) without knowing what will come, and our state of ignorance implies as well a lack of control. Historical change (I do not in this case use the word "development," which implies that change is progressive) has given us a world without secure foundations. Not only migrants and refugees but all of us have lost our homes. We can either mourn this or celebrate it; or perhaps, we can attempt to do both in the creative act, as Rilke and others have.

This dual process of mourning and celebration is characteristic not only of art but, in my view, of therapy as well. The client is also in a state of vulnerability. They have the experience of not knowing what is happening to them and, at the same time, of not having control over it. In therapeutic practice, there is a desire to restore to clients an understanding of their life and some degree of control over it. But in order for this to happen, they must give up their previous understanding and means of control so that they can participate in a genuine therapeutic process. In other words, they must voluntarily experience their vulnerability. In this respect, the client resembles the creative artist. In fact, one might say that authentic therapy is a creative act. This is indeed Winnicott's view, not only for the "patient," but for the therapist as well (1971). In Winnicott's experience, the therapist has no power to change his patients, no way to control their experience and make it go where he will. He must give up his need to be in control and instead "trust the process," in Shaun McNiff's phrase (1998). Furthermore, once a genuine therapeutic process has begun, the therapist cannot claim to understand and thereby control what is happening. The process is a chaotic one, and that means it can be understood only after the fact (as the science of chaos tells us is characteristic of all chaotic processes). Indeed, the therapist's need to understand often is strongest when chaos is most present. Winnicott understands interpretation sometimes to be a way to assuage the therapist's own anxiety at not being able to know and control what is happening.

The therapeutic process, for Winnicott, is analogous to the creative state. It involves a necessary dissolving of the rigid boundaries in the patient's psyche in order for new forms to emerge. In other words, it is an improvisational process, as is artistic creation. Winnicott was, as I have said, a pediatrician before he became a psychoanalyst. He examined thousands of children (some say ten thousand), usually in the company of their mothers, and he observed the back-and-forth play in which child and mother engage. From this, he drew the conclusion that play was the way in which the child could best express itself. The child's development depends, in great part, on the mother's ability to engage in the play and not to make it serve her own needs.

The self, then, emerges in childhood play. Winnicott saw play as an essential element in adult life as well. Play, for him, is the basis of all creativity. Adult play, far from being regressive, is the only way to go forward into the new. In this sense, play can be taken as a model for the psychotherapeutic relationship. The job of the therapist, Winnicott said, is to play with the patient, and if the patient is unable to play, then the therapist's job was to help him learn to play. This, of course, implies that the therapist must be able to play in the first place, something which cannot be taken for granted.

Winnicott's thinking reminds me of the work of Johan Huizinga in his book, *Homo Ludens* (the human as player, as opposed to *homo sapiens*, the human as knower) (1949). Huizinga tries to show that play is at the heart of all culture. Cultural development is founded on our ability to play. One could go further than this and say that play is at the heart of human existence. Only when we play are we authentically human. This seems a far cry from Heidegger's concept of the experience of dread ("*Angst*") that accompanies the realization of our mortality, a dread that we try desperately to avoid.

Indeed, the creative act can be both an experience of mourning and of celebration. It can hold both dread and joy. *Poiesis* is, perhaps, the only act which comes close to expressing both our mortality and our natality. In that sense, perhaps we should change Rilke's sentence "*Gesang ist Dasein*" ("song is existence," my translation) (1985, first published 1923) to "*Dasein ist Gesang*" ("existence is song"). Not only do we truly exist only when we create, but our very existence itself is creative. However, to experience this, we must accept the vulnerability which makes creativity not only possible but necessary.

Human beings are essentially vulnerable not only in our finitude but also in the vulnerability in which we come into the world. We enter the world in a prolonged state of dependency; our self-sufficiency is achieved only through the cultural means of survival which we are taught by others. Unlike other species, we are not pre-adapted to a specific environment. Rather we must invent our means of survival by modifying the environment to satisfy our needs. In other words, we must be creative in order to survive.

This does not, in the first place, depend on our own personal creativity. Rather, we have been handed down the results of creative acts that have been carried out by our forebears. However, as the environment changes and as our needs change with them, we must create new forms that can adequately respond to these changes. These forms may themselves be destructive, in the sense that they bring misery to ourselves, to others and to the world, but new forms must happen. It is then left to future generations to pay the price or reap the benefits.

In a similar way, the creative act and the therapeutic process each contain both destructive and creative aspects. Artists in our time indeed must, in Pound's phrase, "make it new," which means they must destroy the old to make room for what is coming. Similarly, clients must be willing to let go of their past in order to move into a new and more satisfying life. This is difficult work; we tend to cling to what we already have, even if it prolongs our suffering, rather than face the terror of the unknown. It is only through the "holding" that the therapist provides that we can encounter the emptiness that awaits us. Only then can we find the faith that this emptiness may be a creative void.

What then of trauma? How can the perspective we have outlined help us to respond to the traumatic experience, whether it be our own or that of others? In the first place, we have to see trauma as exposing the universal condition of vulnerability in which we all share. There is no possibility of living without being vulnerable. Therefore, we cannot hope to restore the trauma victim to a state of invulnerability; there is no "original nature" to go back to. Rather, traumatized individuals or communities must learn to accept their vulnerability and not attempt to reject it through denial and projection onto others (as the typical abuser does in seeing the other person as responsible for his rage, and as the aggressive nation understands itself to be the victim, not the perpetrator, of violence).

Further, we see helping professionals as sharing in the experience of the victim of trauma through their own essential vulnerability. We cannot stand outside the experience of those who suffer, as observers and agents who are able to control the process of change. Rather we have to find a way to join with others that will give them some sense of their own capacity for authentic life. The path of *poiesis* is one way to do this. If we engage in serious play together, we can move away from the experience of victimhood, and also from the consequent attempt to deny it, into a mutuality that helps us share together both our sorrow and our joy. This experience is necessarily a creative one, whether it results in an art-work or not.

The art of trauma, then, is an engagement in *poiesis* that helps us say, "Yes!" to existence. The vain attempt of Faust to find the one moment to which we can say, "Stay, thou art fair," must give way to an affirmation of human existence in all its dimensions, beautiful and ugly, joyful and horrific. Only such an affirmation can do justice to our ability to go on living creatively in the dreadful face of history. The art of trauma is rooted in the *poiesis* at the very heart of human existence.

LOVE AND BONES

This morning I heard their voices coming through your words
Laughter, tears, the dense hubbub of family close and entwined
Then the screams as they are carried away
And the echoes accompanying you throughout your life

Where are they now?
Baubie, Uncle Jack, your father Abraham?
What happened to Spadina Avenue
Now covered with Chinese restaurants and streetcars screech?

I think of you in Vancouver surrounded by mountains and sea
Protected but not from pain or accident
Protected by words that come to you from the past
That come now to us through you

Ashes into syllables
Skeletons into words
History turned poetry at last

Twisted poet, sing on!
And may your love overcome the smoke and bones
Your song enshrine the memories of what is lost

14

HOPE FOR *POIESIS*

AN INTERVIEW

THE EUROPEAN GRADUATE SCHOOL, JULY 2018

Paolo Knill: My wonder is always, when you entered the field of Expressive Arts at Lesley University in the 1980s, you brought in a word that still today makes things understandable that were not easily explained otherwise, and the word was *poiesis*. I want to introduce that word into our conversation. I imagine you were involved in the arts before. Was the word *poiesis* already there and you brought it together with the arts? Or was it found through your activity?

Stephen K. Levine: When I was in university as an undergraduate, I was a poet and edited the university literary magazine. I wanted to understand what I was doing and the significance that the arts had for me and for human life in general. Later I did my dissertation in philosophy on Heidegger's essay, "The Origin of the Work of Art" (1975, first published 1950). In that essay, he uses the word *poiesis* as a central concept.

From there it seemed to fit into my work in psychotherapy where I was using so-called "action techniques," and into my work in theatre and poetry as well. But it wasn't until I came to Lesley University as a post-doctoral fellow and met you, Paolo, that I had the sense that I could bring all these things together. I was able to do that partly because you recognized the importance of the philosophical dimension in this field.

Previously I had been living in three worlds: in university I was dwelling in philosophy, in theatre in the world of performance, and in therapy in the world of feelings and emotions. When I went to Lesley, I originally thought I would study psychodrama because of my theatre background, but Shaun McNiff, the Dean at that time, said that there was someone I should meet before I decided. That, of course, was you. We had lunch and you immediately started talking about Heidegger; then I knew I was in the right program, where I could do therapy, art and philosophy all together. *Poiesis* is a central word for Heidegger, but I'm not sure whether I stick to his meaning or not.

Over the years I've tried to develop the word in a different direction. Certainly Heidegger didn't have a sense of the therapeutic or social change aspect of *poiesis*. It was used by him solely in reference to the work of art. In the 1970s, when I started studying psychotherapy, I found that the field was understood as self-expression; the goal of therapy and of arts therapy in particular was to express yourself. And, as you and I started working together, I realized art is not self-expression. The art-work is not the self. Perhaps it says something very important for the self, but it is not a reflection or a representation of the self. I think Heidegger's concept of *poiesis* captured that dimension of it.

As my thinking developed in this field, I began to understand the complex nature of the role of *poiesis* in human experience in general, not only in the arts. It has to do with taking what you receive and shaping it in a new direction. Thus, the concept has both a receptive and an active aspect to it. And, in order to work like that, you have to be willing to give up certain things. In particular, you have to be willing to give up control. I remember you often used to say, "You have to give up control in order to achieve mastery." I took that to heart. You have to give up control, and you have to give up knowing in advance what the result will be. And yet these two things, knowing and willing, are the hallmarks of human activity. Human beings are not pre-adapted to a particular environment, rather they have to shape their environment in order to survive. They do so through what Freud understood as the ego functions of knowing and willing. These, then, are considered to be the central characteristics of being human, and also of the divine. God is the paragon of omniscience and omnipotence; He is all-knowing and all-powerful.

However, in order to engage in a poietic act, you have to let go of knowing, and you have to let go of controlling. That's scary and counterintuitive, but I think it is essential in all creative work. *Poiesis* became my way of understanding the work that we do in the field of expressive arts, not in the sense of self-expression but of forming works which then speak to us in meaningful ways.

PK: I may be jumping now to a very different point.

SKL: Jump!

PK: OK. This shaping that happens on condition that you give up control and knowing that produces a work. Perhaps it's a process to get there; however, I cannot imagine anything else when I say giving up control and knowing, then something else becomes present…

SKL: Yes, something else arrives. You have called it the "Third."

PK: Today I would like to say, the work arrives. You are someone who continuously has shown that you are fully aware that although you may have to give up control, however, you do not have to give up skill.

SKL: Right.

PK: You also were one of the scholars I have seen passing through Lesley who got into painting, refining your skills, you even took courses. And still today you take Butoh courses, you take clown courses, voice courses. So what is it that enables us to give up control and knowledge in order to get skills?

SKL: As you know, we have this idea of "low skill/high sensitivity." That is a good slogan for the helping relationship to another person. We don't insist that they become masters in order to paint but that they can paint or be engaged in any other art form through being sensitive to the materials. However, I think that it's important for everyone who is a helper in the field of expressive arts to be skilled in at least one area of art-making so that they have some sense of what it is to make works and how important that is. And, at the same time, the most highly-skilled person has to let go, has to say, "Let's see what's coming," because skill will not produce what does not exist. This is the really difficult part.

Once something comes, of course, you can shape and refine it and use your skills to achieve a result. At that point, your reflective capacity comes in, your knowing, because the work is coming, but then you step back and reflect on it: Did it arrive? What does it need? And then you can engage with it again. That's one of the things I learned from you about so-called "takes," the idea that you can keep working on something until the work arrives. You don't have to just say, "Let's dance," and then ask, "How was that? How did you feel?" The question is much more one of asking, "Did it arrive? Does it work?" And, if not, "What would you need to make it arrive?" or, "Let's do it again and here's a suggestion for you." Perhaps I see something in a movement sequence, for example, and I say: "Don't forget, you can use different levels, you can go fast or slow, you can be sharp or smooth in your movements," and so forth. So, the more I know, the more I can help someone with letting something new arrive. However, I can't produce it. I can't make it. And that's what's scary about the arts. That's why we have writer's block and stage fright, because it really is a question of going into a place of unknowing and a lack of control. And that is opposite to the way we live—even me, I like to know what's going on and I like to be in charge of it.

Recently, I was going to write a poem about an illness that I had been diagnosed with, inspired by the dissertation of Irene Renzenbrink at EGS, who talks about working with loss through the arts (2018). So I thought, OK, I'll start with that. I began with that impulse, then suddenly there was a connection in the poem with the people who were at the border in the United States who were being mistreated, jailed and separated from their children. This situation seemed somehow connected with my need to accept what comes. Do I accept my loss? Do we accept them? How can we do this? Acceptance is counter to all our impulses, which are to keep away things that may be bad and bring in only good things. But, sometimes you have to say: "I let in whatever comes." The poem was a big surprise to me, that it had anything to do with the border situation in the United States, which I was not thinking about at all, but which of course I had been very concerned with, as have many people, the horrible ways in which refugees and immigrants are treated. The separation of children from their parents is a notorious crime, so it must have been on my mind in some sense. And it popped up in this poem about myself and my illness.

Shall I read you the poem?

PK: Yes.

SKL: As I said, I had been given a diagnosis of Parkinson's disease, a motor disorder. It's quite troubling, and I had difficulty accepting the diagnosis. My wife, Ellen Levine, and I decided we would call it "Mr. P." That made it seem more familiar, to personalize it, so this poem is called "Welcoming Mr. P."

WELCOMING MR. P

Mr. P is knocking at the door
must I let him in?
He bears no gifts,
only burden, danger, fear,

At the border there are others
no better than us
or even worse,
must we let them in?

"You shall welcome the stranger
for you were once a stranger yourself"
It does not say,
"welcome the stranger
who will give you what you need"

I hear him knock
I hear them knocking
I am knocking too
Welcoming
what comes

It was a total surprise to me that coming to terms with my illness through the arts would have anything to do with the way people are treated at the United States border with Mexico, and at the borders of other countries too in this worldwide refugee crisis.

PK: And, at the same time, you quote yourself in a strange way. For me, it is the most important statement you ever made about *poiesis*, and you did it repeatedly. I remember that it was in your first book, *Poiesis: The Language of Psychology and the Speech of the Soul* (1997). You read this statement to the community in the community meeting as an important finding.

SKL: What was that?

PK: Guess.

SKL: I don't know! The one statement that keeps recurring to me is in the essay I wrote for *Foundations of Expressive Arts Therapy* (1999), "*Poiesis* is always possible," but I don't think that's the one you mean.

PK: That is a great one, but it's not the one I mean. The one I mean is: "Bringing gifts to the feast" (Levine, 1997).

SKL: That's true. Of course, in that case I was talking about when someone brings you a gift, you welcome it without any problem. If someone wants to bring me a gift, I like it, but, if someone comes to the door, and I don't know whether they are bringing a gift or not, I become wary. Many people in our field would like to turn a disaster into a gift: "Oh, you have this disease, well, there are so many things you can do, maybe it will help you in the end." But sometimes it's not a gift, or it's a gift in the sense in which *das Gift* in German means "the poison." You don't know what's coming, and to welcome that is much more difficult than when someone says "Here's your birthday present!"

PK: You said in another context that the gift you bring may be, I'm pretty sure I'm quoting, "Tears and other difficult feelings."

SKL: Ha! Well, I would agree with that. I don't know that I said it that exact way, but I definitely agree. Yes, when someone cries in a group, I always say to them, if you feel ashamed, realize that this is a gift you are giving to the group. It allows us to connect with your distress and sorrow and that allows us to connect to our own sorrow. In fact, I will say this about the "gift" of Mr. P, who I don't think of as bringing gifts really, but it enabled me to connect with the suffering of the refugees, which I wasn't really thinking about at all, so in that sense, it's true. And I think it's a Buddhist perspective also. I understand when Buddhists say existence is suffering, because we always want to hold on to what is, rather than accept that everything is passing, and that we suffer from not letting go. They also say that if you can accept this transitory nature of existence, you feel great compassion for all beings. I think that's it exactly.

PK: Including the shaped beings.

SKL: Ah, ha! Say more about that.

PK: In helping people and in leading them through a process, we use the image in the way you describe. It's as if the image is as much waiting for you as you are waiting for it.

SKL: Absolutely.

PK: So, in that statement it's evident that in order that it can arrive, you use your skills.

SKL: Yes, we help it to arrive with skill.

PK: You say there is something in treatment that is similar to this perspective. It needs skills to treat people. And one skill is that you serve whatever needs to come.

SKL: Whatever needs to come, you help it to arrive. I like to refer to Socrates, who said that the job of the philosopher is not to tell you the truth, but to be a midwife to your ideas. To help you arrive at your own ideas, give birth to them. I don't think Plato took that statement too seriously himself, but I think it's a brilliant idea.

PK: To make such a statement and guiding thought, you must have had the experience of working with the arts. You are a living example of these thoughts based on your experience. So you have done art and you train in art, and thus you can make the thing come faster. You still train for it, but what motivates you then? You especially. Writers write books and books. Like Sisyphus, they do it again and again.

SKL: Yes, again and again, because you're never finished. Sometimes I worry that I'm repeating myself, and I probably am. I think I have one idea about *poiesis* and just keep repeating it over and over—but that is probably what most philosophers do. They have an idea, and just keep saying it in different ways and seeing different aspects of it. I think for me, part of it is you have to love philosophy. Certainly, this is true in theatre; otherwise why would I keep taking these workshops? Sometimes I can't do them very well, but at the same time that I hate it, I love it. Doing Butoh is a good example—everyone in the class is a trained dancer and about 40–50 years younger than me (laughter), so I am always thinking, "Oh I'm so clumsy, I'm not doing this well." I remember saying to my Butoh teacher, Denise Fujiwara, "I suck at Butoh!" She looked at me and said, after a moment's pause, "Well, you're improving" (laughter). And I love that because she didn't say: "Oh no, you're very good." We both knew that wasn't true. But there is something about doing it, I don't know what it is, the sense of discovery maybe, the sense that something may be arriving that I didn't know was there before. That's what all creative work is in a way, giving birth. It's scary, but also very satisfying. Of course, sometimes it's a stillbirth, or it even produces a monster. Sometimes it's a failure, but when something does happen, it's a great pleasure. So I think that's the joy in it.

PK: Something still bugs me. We can get lost by going into explanations, that the sculpture is already there, we have to peel it out of the stone to reveal it, etc. Yes, sure it needs skill in order to help it come through, but can I really help it if it is so powerful? Does it help itself? So what exactly is this activity we do when you describe these things? I believe that you have experienced them. But when Heidegger writes about them for instance, he may write poetry, but I don't see him doing Butoh.

SKL: There are several things about that that I want to say. First of all, Heidegger is a language person and was part of the linguistic turn in philosophy. I don't think he is really familiar with any of the other arts. In the essay, "The Origin of the Work of Art" (1975, first published 1950), he does an analysis of a painting by Van Gogh, the one of two boots. It's a beautiful phenomenological analysis, but it's also very imaginative, and he's been criticized for interpreting the two boots in the painting as peasant boots. He imagines the world of the peasant woman in the fields and then her bringing in the boots with mud on them, and how they support her experience of her world. But I also read an interpretation of that painting by a psychoanalyst who said something like this (I've forgotten the source): "It's Van Gogh's own boot. If you see that one of the boots has a shoelace that lies on the other, then you realize that this is the painting of two brothers, Vincent and Theo. The shoelace that lies on the other shows that Vincent is relying on Theo. Each of the boots represents one brother." This seems to me to totally ignore the aesthetic quality of the work. Heidegger does go into an imaginative interpretation in his phenomenological analysis, but at least he had some sense of the beauty of Van Gogh's painting. His examples otherwise are mostly drawn from poetry, particularly the work of Hölderlin, with a little bit of Rilke, Stefan George, and so forth.

The amazing thing to me is that Heidegger's writing on the poets is so sensitive. He is receptive to what they have to offer, but on the other hand he's such a shit when it comes to human beings. Remember, he was an anti-Semite and a follower of Hitler. His *Black Notebooks* (2017, first published 2014) have recently become available. These were private journals he kept. We see in them that he was not only a follower of Hitler publicly, but privately throughout his life, he was an anti-Semite. How can that be? Ezra Pound was the same. How can you be a fascist and still be a poet? This is peculiar. It's like there is a different dimension of your life than the one that comes out in your work. Since most people identify the work with the person, they can't accept this contradiction. They either say Heidegger never was a fascist, or that his philosophical writing is crap because of his politics. I don't think either one of those is the truth. He was a terrible human being and a wonderful philosopher. If we judged people's works by who they are, we would then have to say that a good person produces a good work and a bad person produces a bad work. That's obviously not true.

PK: It would be totally against the point of view of expressive arts.

SKL: Totally against reality. Heidegger's case is very strange, particularly because his work is really all about letting go, letting be, *Seinlassen*—the opposite of fascism, which was based on "the triumph of the will," to quote the title of the film about one of Hitler's rallies in Nuremberg.

PK: And nowadays…

SKL: Well, Trump is a good example of the triumph of the will. For him, if I want it, it's true. And if I want it, it must exist. And anything that prevents me from getting what I want is bad and needs to be destroyed. This is terrible!

PK: Hypothetically, can you imagine rewriting the whole philosophy of our world view, the *Menschenbild*, of Expressive Arts as built on *poiesis*? Is there something else that needs to be said today? Something to be changed in the foundation of our field?

SKL: Well, I'm sure that someone else will change it, and that's good. But as for me, I stand by this. I also feel like I need to keep thinking things through and consider all the different aspects. For example, one of the things I've been thinking about a lot is that in psychotherapy, outside of Expressive Arts, there has been a tremendous interest in the past decades on relational work, so-called "relational psychotherapy." I'm wondering, what is the importance of the relationship in Expressive Arts and in art-making generally? I think of Cathy Moon's book *Studio Art Therapy* (2001). She has an excellent chapter on relationship in the arts therapies.

I have come to understand that art is relational in its essence. Sometimes we still have a hangover from the modern concept of the artist as an isolated genius, who creates out of his… his own mind. I emphasize the masculine pronoun because it's not a traditionally feminine perspective, which emphasizes relationship. I think we have to reinsert our thinking about the arts into understanding our existence as a being with others, Heidegger says this well in *Being and Time* (1962), that what is existential about human existence is *Mit-sein* (being with) and *In-der-welt-sein* (being in the world). We are with others, and art-making takes place in the world with others.

First of all, the work is always coming from me to you, even if the "you" is undefined and may in fact never exist. The poet Paul Celan talks about the poem being a message in a bottle that is sent into the sea and you don't know where it lands. Maybe it's writing "for the drawer" (I think of all the Soviet writers who could not publish), maybe it never sees daylight, maybe it's destroyed. But it could be read, and it's meant to be read. The painting is meant to be seen. That's why I always tell Ellen she has to exhibit more, because her painting needs to be seen. It says: "Look at me, look at me!" And, the poem says: "Read me, hear me!"

I think there is something very relational about *poiesis* to begin with. Furthermore, in the arts every medium is handed down to us from others, even if we destroy it, even if we alter it radically. But we begin with it. And this tradition means something because it is handed down from others. How do we know to paint on a canvas or not to paint on a canvas? Because not to do something is also to have a relationship to it. How do I know that I am writing poetry? My poems might not have been considered poetry a few hundred years ago, when we had to stick to classical models (a sonnet, a sestina, an ode, for example). The whole idea of so-called "free verse," which is not free but that doesn't follow an established metrical pattern, is a new concept developed by others. This relation to the other is true for me as well. I've been very influenced by many other poets, the Beats, Allen Ginsberg, as well as poets like Celan, Rilke, all of the great poets.

PK: Am I hopefully not far from your imagination about *poiesis* when I say that it is based on resonance and that art is always in resonance in a relationship.

SKL: I like this idea of resonance, but I would have to think more about it. It's not my concept, but I like it. We say in music, if you want to make music, the first thing you have to do is listen. And if you're making music with others, you definitely have to listen to the resonance between their sound and yours. We have to think also about attunement, as Mitchell Kossak says (2015). How am I attuned to the other? Do I resonate with what the other has to say, even if I disagree with it? I need to think more about to what degree *poiesis* is a matter of resonance, even when the resonance involves dissonance.

PK: For me, the thinking of *poesis* is not different from the perspective based on resonance. The resonance principle comes for me as a musician, and as a community artist, I cannot avoid that people hear each other. They may not listen, but they hear each other. They're forced to deal with resonance and non-resonance. They are only in the world in relationship to what was already done, what will be done.

SKL: Definitely!

PK: So, the whole focus on community art and this so-called "performance art," a key word today in exhibits, also brings the discourse to the level of *poiesis*, you do it and you witness it.

SKL: Yes, there is always a witness to every performance. Hans Georg Gadamer, in his book *Truth and Method* (2004) says that every work of art is a performance, including painting. The painting only exists when someone is looking at it, so in that sense it is performing itself through your vision. I think this is a very profound insight of his. Ultimately it's all performance.

Of course, you have brought so much into our field, including the notion of community art which is so strong and which leads us not only to do this work here at EGS with students and faculty, but also to work in communities, to do social change work. We use the same principles of community art in all community work that aims at change. That was a great gift. I think your great contribution was to stand on this principle that art is about making, shaping, and it's about wanting the work. The poet wants the poem, the musician wants the music. They don't want to just express themselves. We wait for it to arrive and we do our best to shape it when it comes, but it does not express the self. In fact, it gets us out of the preoccupation with the self.

First of all, the focus on the self in isolation is a great disease of individualism, and is itself tied up with capitalism and the competitive market system. It also has to do with the whole philosophical system we've inherited from Descartes, where individuals are cut off not only from their bodies but from others and from the world. Most of psychology has inherited this perspective, which I think is a total disaster. In a way, your work as an artist and in music and community art has brought us back into this relationship to the world and to the other, which we are often missing in the arts therapies.

PK: So your skill-training that you never get tired of is actually nothing else than a kind of dynamic meditation in becoming aware that art is living in this concept of relationship.

SKL: Yes, even when the relationship is a mess, as relationships often are.

PK: So even though a therapist may not do art with a client, they should make art for themselves to exercise this capacity.

SKL: That's an interesting point. I would say, going back to your definition, that therapy is always an "art analogue" process, even if the arts are not directly involved. It's the same process when the therapist is receptive, does not force something on the client. There is so much therapy today, because of insurance and general tendencies in the culture, in which you are supposed to give a solution within six sessions. In Ellen Levine's workplace, they are even working on single sessions. Single session therapy, this is insane! In such a case, you as a therapist must have an agenda, and you want to push this agenda on your client. It's terrible, because I think the essence of therapy is the receptive attitude. How can I help you bring out what is within you? That's education. That was the original meaning of *educare*, to bring out what is already there. That requires skill, patience and holding your own needs at bay. It's very satisfying, but you can't make it your agenda.

Recently, a young woman from Peru wrote to me. She was in dire straits. I immediately became concerned for her, wrote to the teachers in Peru and told them to contact her, to help her. What happened when she found out about this was that she was furious with me and said: "I didn't ask for your help, I don't want people to do that." And, eventually, I apologized profusely. We're all subject to this need to fix it, to have people not suffer. I was afraid she might hurt herself. But my intervention was not helpful. I realized there was some counter-transference, as we say, and there was a need of my own to rescue her. So, it happens to everyone.

PK: Can you give a little comment on the following: You said we are there to help them express what is within them.

SKL: Not "express," to help them discover or uncover what is within them. Heidegger's philosophy depends on the notion of truth as uncovering, not as correspondence between statement and fact. He goes back to the Greek word *aletheia*, which means literally "bringing out of darkness." *Lethe* is the river of darkness, the river that leads you when you die. Truth is not the correspondence between a statement and an objective state of affairs, which is the usual concept of truth. For example, I see that this table in front of me is brown. When I make the statement, "This table is brown," I see that the actuality of this state of affairs corresponds, therefore this statement is true.

Heidegger says, on the other hand, that this is a secondary notion of truth (1962, p.260). The fundamental sense is that there is a table in the first place. To have a table, you must already live in a world in which tables exist, you have already inherited meaning where what it means to be a table is already uncovered. Truth as uncovering also means there is always more that is yet to be uncovered. We don't say that this "more" is in the unconscious, which means nothing in my opinion, all that means is I don't know where it is, it is *Unbewusstsein* (unknown). The word "unconscious" in English means the same thing as the German, not-knowing. And it's true, we may not yet know something, but that doesn't mean that it is in me, "in my head." I need to discover it.

We're in a very bad situation right now in the world. My only hope is that new creative possibilities that are not apparent can be uncovered. Heidegger (1993, first published 1954) quotes the poet Hölderlin, who said: "But where danger is, grows the saving power also…" And I think that might be part of what he meant. That out of this disaster there may be something we're not aware of that is trying to be born. Let's welcome it and hope that it arrives.

When I say *poiesis* is always possible, I believe it—but I'm not sure it's true, if that makes any sense. Because I can conceive of many situations, extreme situations, where maybe it's not possible.

PK: That would be sad, because then it would be possible to stop everything.

SKL: Yes, to stop everything. It's a little like *Remnants of Auschwitz*, Giorgio Agamben's beautiful book on the meaning of Auschwitz (2002). He writes about what the prisoners in Auschwitz called the "*Muselmann*." That's actually a racist designation because the word literally means Muslim. What they were trying to say, without knowing how to say it, is that sometimes prisoners lose so much hope and so much capacity to act that they look like someone who is bowing up and down at prayer without any volition, without any intention. It's an automatic thing, as close to being dead as you can be and still be alive, without any capacity to respond.

I don't know, though, is that true? Even in Auschwitz there was theatre, there was music. Elie Wiesel's book, *Night* (2012, first published 1958), a beautiful book that I recommend to everybody, talks about how on a forced march at the end of the war, there was one man who had a violin and had been commanded to play for the Nazis in the camp. When the prisoners stopped for the night and lay down, he started to play of his own volition. He played beautifully, and then he died. It was his last act before he died. All the prisoners heard this, and it gave them some hope in the world.

So, I don't know. Is *poiesis* always possible? What if we were to act as if it were always possible? This is the philosophy of "as if" by Hans Vaihinger, as he outlines it in his book of that title (2009, first published 1925)—you may have come across it.

PK: I think of *Spielraum*, the play range. As if the play range were always there.

SKL: Yes, as if the play range were always there. Can you actually eliminate it? In the wonderful book, *Resistance: My Life for Lebanon*, by Souha Bechara (2003), the author talks about the time she was in prison in Lebanon because she had tried to assassinate a fascist leader in that country. She was captured and sent to this infamous prison where they were tortured and deprived of everything; but the women prisoners were together and would make little figures out of thread from their clothes and dust from the floor. That's all they had. They would create little creatures and make worlds where there was nothing, absolutely nothing. It was as close to nothing you can get without being in a sensory deprivation tank, and they still made art.

PK: And challenged themselves with skill.

SKL: Yes, skill. It's not so easy to make little sculptures out of dust and thread. So, I hope that *poiesis* is always possible, and I hope it will be possible for me because otherwise I can give way to despair. Actually, what helped me with the poem I read before about my illness was that Irene's dissertation had inspired me by all the examples she gave of people, including herself, who had lost everything, but were still able not only to go on living, but also to give birth to something new. So we encourage each other. I think that's very important. Not that everything is wonderful and we're all going to be happy, and expressive arts therapy will solve the world's problems, but that it's always possible to give a poietic response.

PK: If only Expressive Arts could help to reduce all this chatter about self-expression and turn it into a discourse on training skills.

SKL: Yes, we need skill, but we need hope first of all. My hope is that our community will support each of us in finding not only the will to live but also the will to create. My fervent belief is that *poiesis* can lead us to a better life for all.

SONG THE ONLY VICTORY

Poets have always been prize-winners
and losers. The bardic contest
a precursor to the cutting sessions
of forties jazz.
Even tragedy had its laureate.
No solemnity there,
when the victory banquet
lasted until dawn.
Now we enter slams,
sing out for votes in coffee houses,
clip coupons and send in
twenty-dollar checks.
The divine vocation always coupled with ambition:
To be the chosen one, immortal
for a moment, gloriously-crowned
before the fall.

So when I voted for myself,
instead of the 12-year old's
poems of the Holocaust,
I was in good company.
And in the bar later, Nicole's words,
"You were my favorite poet," lifted me up
for one moment, no matter how absurd,
raised me to the pantheon of bards.

I remember the wreath I wore in Saas Fee,
fashioned by the students for us all.
How close to crown of thorns!
It hung on my closet door until
the leaves were withered and brown.

Words remain. They
prick us
and we bleed.
Signs of life when
we are gone.
Even after Auschwitz?
Yes, I say yes,
we sing on
hoping to be heard.
The whole mad medley bursting into song.
The ashes, blood, sex,
little vanities of soul,
all remembered
in the poem.

And if there is no deliverance, no
ultimate judge who will forgive,
then keep on singing, keep
delivering your words, sending them
into the world, a privilege
to be heard, to make the common speech
a publicity.

Poets, singers of the city,
I salute you, crown you
with these words, greet you
as brothers and sisters,
companions at the feast.
Let us celebrate
even as we fail,
even as darkness surrounds us
and silence claims the earth.
Sing on, my company.
Song is the only victory.
Sing on, I say,
O yes,
Sing on.

REFERENCES

Adorno, T. (1967) *Prisms*. London: Neville Spearman.

Agamben, G. (2002) *Remnants of Auschwitz: The Witness and the Archive*. Cambridge, MA: Zone Books.

American Psychiatric Association (2013) *Diagnostic and Statistical Manual of Mental Disorders* (DSM). Washington: American Psychiatric Association Publishing.

Arendt, H. (1958) *The Human Condition*. Chicago: The University of Chicago Press. (Original work published 1958).

Bechara, S. (2003) *Resistance: My Life for Lebanon*, Trans. G. Levine. Brooklyn, NY: Soft Skull Press.

Becker, E. (1997) *The Denial of Death*. New York: Free Press.

Bloom, H. (1997) *The Anxiety of Influence*. New York: Oxford University Press. (Original work published 1973).

Butler, J. (2014) *Parting Ways: Jewishness and the Critique of Zionism*. New York: Columbia University Press.

Castoriadis, C. (1998) *The Imaginary Institution of Society*. Boston: MIT Press.

Celan, P. (1999) "Speech on the Occasion of Receiving the Literaure Prize of the Free Hanseatic City of Bremen." In *Collected Prose*. Trans. R. Waldrop. Manchester: Carcanet. (Original work published 1958).

Chuang Tzu (1964) *Chuang Tzu: Basic Writings*. Trans. B. Watson. New York: Columbia University Press.

Coetzee, J.M. (1999) *The Lives of Animals*. Princeton, New Jersey: Princeton University Press.

Coetzee, J.M. (2003*) Elizabeth Costello*. New York: Viking.

Coleridge, S. (1997) *The Complete Poems*. London: Penguin.

Darwish, M. (2007) "Edward Said: A Contrapuntal Reading." *Cultural Critique*, 67, 175–182.

Derrida, J. (1973) *Speech and Phenomena*. Evanston, IL: Northwestern University Press.

Derrida, J. (2005*) Rogues: Two Essays on Reason*. Stanford, CA: Stanford University Press.

Derrida, J. (2008) *The Animal That Therefore I Am*. New York: Fordham University Press.

Eberhart, H. and Atkins, S. (2014) *Presence and Process in Expressive Arts Work: At the Edge of Wonder*. London: Jessica Kingsley Publishers.

Ferlinghetti, L. (2007) *Poetry as Insurgent Art*. New York: New Directions.

Gadamer, H. (2004) *Truth and Method*. London: Continuum.

Goethe, J.W.V. (2014) *Faust*. London: Yale University Press. (Original work published in 1808).

Haider, A. (2018) *Mistaken Identity: Race and Class in the Age of Trump*. London: Verso.

Haraway, D. (2003) *The Companion Species Manifesto: Dogs, People and Significant Otherness*. Chicago: Prickly Paradigm Press.

Hardt, M. and Negri, A. (2004) *Multitude: War and Democracy in the Age of Empire*. New York: The Penguin Press.

Heidegger, M. (1962) *Being and Time*. Trans. J. Macquarrie and E. Robinson. New York: Harper. (Original work published 1926).

Heidegger, M. (1975) "The Origin of the Work of Art." In *Poetry, Language, Thought*. New York: Harper. (Original work published 1950).

Heidegger M. (1993) "The Question Concerning Technology." In *Basic Writings*. Trans. D. Krell. New York: Harper. (Original work published 1954).

Heidegger, M. (2002) *Off the Beaten Path*. Trans. J. Young and K. Haynes. Cambridge, UK: Cambridge University Press. (Original work published 1950).

Heidegger, M. (2017) *Ponderings VII–XI: Black Notebooks 1938–1939*. Trans. R. Rojcewicz. Bloomington, Indiana: Indiana University Press. (Original work published 2014).

Hillman, J. (1977) "An Inquiry into Image." *Spring: An Annual of Archeypal Psychology and Jungian Thought*, 62–68.

Hillman, J (1992) *We've had 100 Years of Psychotherapy—and the World's Getting Worse*. New York: Harper.

Hillman, J. (1999) *The Force of Character: And the Lasting Life*. New York: Ballantine Books.

Hillman, J. (1983) *Archetypal Psychology: Uniform Edition of the Writings of James Hillman, Vol 1*. Washington: Spring Publications.

Huizinga, J. (1949) *Homo Ludens: A Study of the Play Element in Culture*. London: Routledge.

Jullien, F. (2016) *This Strange Idea of the Beautiful*. London: Seagull Press.

Kafka, F. (2013) *Report for an Academy*. Trans. I. Johnston. Kartindo Publishing House.

Kalman, M. (2007) *The Principles of Uncertainty*. New York: The Penguin Press.

Kant, I. (1951) *Critique of Judgement*. Trans. J. Bernard. New York: Hafner. (Original work published 1790).

Keats. J. (1899) *The Complete Poetical Works and Letters of John Keats: Cambridge Edition*. Boston and New York: Houghton, Mifflin and Company.

Kierkegaard, S. (1999) *The Living Thoughts of Kierkegaard*. New York: New York Review of Books.

Knill, P., Levine, E. and Levine, S. (2005) *Principles and Practice of Expressive Arts Therapy: Toward a Therapeutic Aesthetics*. London: Jessica Kingsley Publishers.

Kossak, M. (2015) *Attunement in Expressive Arts Therapy: Toward an Understanding of Embodied Empathy*. Springfield, IL: Charles C. Thomas.

Lenfestey, J. (2007) *A Cartload of Scrolls: 100 Poems in the Manner of T'ang Dynasty Poet Han Shan*. Duluth, MN: Holy Cow Press.

Levinas, E. (1991) *Totality and Infinity*. Dordrecht, The Netherlands: Kluwer Academic Publishers.

Levinas, E. (1998) *Otherwise than Being or Beyond Essence*. Pittsburgh: Duquesne University.

Levine, S. (1997) *The Language of Psychology and the Speech of the Soul*. London: Jessica Kingsley Publishers.

Levine, S. (1999) "*Poiesis* and Post-modernism: The Search for a Foundation in Expressive Arts Therapy." In S. Levine and E. Levine (eds) *Foundations of Expressive Arts Therapy: Theoretical and Clinical Perspectives.* London: Jessica Kingsley Publishers.

Levine, S. (2009) *Trauma, Tragedy, Therapy: The Arts and Human Suffering.* London: Jessica Kingsley Publishers.

Levine, S. (2017) "Nature as a Work of Art." In E. Levine and S. Levine (eds) *New Developments in Expressive Arts Therapy: The Play of Poiesis.* London: Jessica Kingsley Publishers.

Levine, S. and Levine, E. (eds) (1999) *Foundations of Expressive Arts Therapy: Theoretical and Clinical Perspectives,* London: Jessica Kingsley Publishers.

Levine, E., and Levine, S. (eds) (2011) *Art in Action: Expressive Arts Therapy and Social Change,* London: Jessica Kingsley Publishers.

Marx, W. (1987) *Is There a Measure on Earth?* Chicago: The University of Chicago Press. (Original work published 1983).

McNiff, S. (1998) *Trust the Process.* Boston: Shambhala.

McNiff, S. (2004) *Art Heals: How Creativity Cures the Soul.* Boston: Shambhala.

Merleau-Ponty, M. (1973) *The Prose of the World.* Trans. J. O'Neill. Evanston, IL: Northwestern University Press. (Original work published 1969).

Moon, C.H. (2002) *Studio Art Therapy: Cultivating the Artist Identity in the Art Therapist.* London: Jessica Kingsley Publishers.

Moreno, J. and Fox, J. (ed.) (1987) *The Essential Moreno.* New York: Springer. (Original work published 1940).

Nancy, J.-L. (2005) The *Ground of the Image.* New York: Fordham University Press.

Nietzsche, F. (1967) *The Birth of Tragedy and the Case of Wagner,* New York: Vintage. (Original work published 1872).

Ong, W. (1982) *Orality and Literacy.* London: Routledge.

Phillips, A. (1988) *Winnicott.* London: Fontana Press.

Pirandello, L. (1960) *Tonight We Improvise.* New York: Samuel French. (Original work published 1930).

Plato (1966) "Phaedo". In *The Last Days of Socrates.* Trans. H. Tredennick. Baltimore: Penguin.

Plato (1987) *The Republic.* Trans. D. Lee. New York: Penguin.

Renzenbrink, I. (2018) "*So Many Little Dyings: Illuminating Loss and Grief Through the Arts.*" Unpublished doctoral dissertation, European Graduate School, Leuk, Switzerland.

Rilke, R. (1985) *Sonnets to Orpheus.* Trans. S. Mitchell. New York: Simon and Shuster. (Original work published 1923).

Shelley, P. (2009) *A Defense of Poetry.* Charleston, SC: BiblioBazaar. (Original work published 1840).

Silberberg, S. (2012) "*Illuminating Liminality: A Collaborative Photo-based Process with People Affected by Marginalization in a Harm Reduction Environment.*" Unpublished doctoral dissertation. European Graduate School, Leuk, Switzerland.

Sinapius, P. (2008) "The Self is an Image." In *POIESIS: A Journal of the Arts and Communication* 10, 92–104.

Slingerland, E. (2000) "Effortless Action: The Chinese Spiritual Ideal of *Wu-wei.*" *Journal of the American Academy of Religion* 68, 2, 293–328.

Thoreau, H.D. (2013) *Walking: Annotated Edition.* St. Louis: J. Missouri. (Original work published 1862).

Turner, V. (1995) *The Ritual Process: Structure and Anti-Structure.* Chicago: Aldine.

Vaihinger, H. (2009) *The Philosophy of "As If"*. Abingdon: Routledge (Original work published in 1925).

Waley, A. (1958) *The Way and Its Power: Lao Tzu's Tao Te Ching and Its Place in Chinese Thought*. New York: Grove Press. (Original work published 1934).

Weller, J. (1993) "Planting Your Feet Firmly in Nothingness." *CREATE: Journal of the Creative and Expressive Arts Therapies Exchange*, 3, 103–109.

Wiesel, E. (2012) *Night*. New York: Hill and Wang. (Original work published in 1958).

Whitehead, A. (1979) *Process and Reality*. New York: Simon and Schuster.

Whitman, W. (2015) *Song of Myself*. Los Angeles: Zephyr House.

Winnicott, D.W. (1974) *Playing and Reality*. Harmondsworth: Penguin. (Original work published 1971)

Wolff, E. (2002) *Treating the Self: Elements of Clinical Self Psychology*. New York: The Guilford Press.

Wood, D. (2002) *Thinking After Heidegger*. Cambridge, UK: Polity Press

Yeats, W. (1959) *The Collected Poems of W. B. Yeats*. New York: Macmillan. (Original work published 1921).

SUBJECT INDEX

AUTHOR INDEX